Praise for

The Future of God

"Being a nuclear physicist dealing with basic quantum field theory, I find my worldview agreeing with Deepak Chopra. The all-embracing holistic quantum field is a step forward from our classical reductionistic interpretation of a determined 'reality.' It suggests a dynamic, alive cosmos, or 'Wirklichkeit.' Dr. Chopra's work will be talked about for a long time to come."

—HANS PETER DUERR, scientific member and director emeritus of Max Planck Institute for Physics and Astrophysics

"As Deepak explains, Dawkins's materialism is the delusion, not God. Eastern spiritualists, Western constructivists, and quantum physicists agree—the mind shapes, if not creates, the world. Materialism is a mirage of deeper level quantum reality, one which surfaces in living systems, guiding consciousness and evolution. The 'Watchmaker' isn't blind. Dawkins is."

—STUART HAMEROFF, M.D., professor of anesthesiology and psychology director of the Center for Consciousness Studies at the University of Arizona, www.quantumconsciousness.org

"*The Future of God* is a brilliant exposition for the need of consciousness-based reality. It is consistent with the worldview of quantum physics that showed the importance of the mind and is a fitting answer to the claims of militant atheists whose science is based on outdated views now known to not be true and which became obsolete almost a century ago."

—MENAS C. KAFATOS, Fletcher Jones Professor of
Computational Physics at Chapman University
and coauthor of *The Non-Local Universe:
The New Physics and Matters of the Mind*

"A magnificent and masterfully argued presentation of why randomness can never explain the great mystery of life on earth. This wonderfully accessible book is a must-read for anyone who, much like Einstein and other pioneers of the new physics did, experiences a feeling of utter humility when contemplating the grandeur of the cosmos."

—P. MURALI DORAISWAMY, professor of psychiatry and
member of the Duke Institute for Brain Sciences.

"Deepak Chopra has successfully blended ancient Vedanta philosophy with his unique perspective on modern science to provide a vast audience with solutions that meet many needs for our modern age. He is among the influential scholars, authors, and thinkers who have found truth in the Perennial philosophy and developed ways to help people apply that truth to their daily lives."

—HUSTON SMITH, author of *Why Religion Matters:
The Fate of the Human Spirit in an Age of Disbelief*

"The most transformative discoveries begin with delusion, are challenged by insight, driven by faith, pursued with science, and culminate in truth. Deepak Chopra beautifully makes the case that the biggest delusion is a universe without God or consciousness."

—RUDY TANZI, coauthor of the
New York Times bestseller *Super Brain*

"At a time when the revolutions of the physical sciences are changing our understanding of the human consciousness, *The Future of God* is a book that needed to be written, and no one could have written it better than Deepak Chopra. In this brilliant analysis, Chopra shows how God is evolving with our consciousness, and how both the religious and atheistic fundamentalists are focused on an outdated God. This book is a treasure of deep insights that will not only touch your heart but will also lead you to understand how a God without illusions is a necessary condition for your physical well-being."

—LOTHAR SCHÄFER, distinguished professor of
physical chemistry (emeritus) at the University
of Arkansas and author of *Infinite Potential*

"In *The Future of God,* Deepak Chopra crisply dissects the militant atheist's assertion that there is no meaning or purpose to life, and no need for faith in an accidental universe. He lays bare the belief vs. disbelief controversy and provides sound reasons why it is both possible and necessary to mature beyond the simplistic dogmas that have sustained a timeworn and increasingly futile debate."

—DEAN RADIN, PH.D., author of
The Conscious Universe and *Supernormal*

"*The Future of God* is a much-needed book. Chopra convincingly exposes the limitations, arrogance, and intellectual blindness of the 'new atheists.' He recognizes that unbelief has a role to play, but he also shows how to go beyond the atheists' narrow dogmatism to a far richer experience and understanding of reality."

—RUPERT SHELDRAKE, PH.D., author of *Science Set Free*

"*The Future of God* is the freshest riposte yet in response to the chest-beating, triumphal, militant atheism that can't stop congratulating itself for imaginary victories over traditional religion. Dr. Chopra shows how this tiresome movement is based in bad philosophy, bad science, and bad psychology, and how it is mired in abysmal confusion about what authentic spirituality is all about. He shows how militant atheism, through sleight of hand, merely substitutes one blind faith for another, managing to fool itself in the process. In *The Future of God,* Dr. Chopra describes an approach to God that is congruent with a modern worldview, while simultaneously honoring the innate human connection with the Divine."

—LARRY DOSSEY, M.D., author of *One Mind: How Our Individual Mind Is Part of a Greater Consciousness and Why It Matters*

"The continuing struggle between two worldviews, one religious, the other scientific, has confused the Western mind enormously. In this book the visionary Deepak Chopra has taken on the task of a 'guide for the perplexed' as only he can. *The Future of God* is important for two reasons. First, and this is marvelous, Deepak has done a wonderful job of debunking the so-called debunkers, people like Richard Dawkins, who, it seems, cannot even distinguish between popular and esoteric aspects of religion. The latter is about spirituality, which has found new support from quantum physics and other recent breakthroughs in science. The second reason for the book's importance is that it really is a reliable guide to why and how you can seek God in even these confusing times."

—AMIT GOSWAMI, quantum physicist and author of *The Self-Aware Universe, The Quantum Doctor,* and *How Quantum Activism Can Save Civilization*

The Future of God

The Future
of God

A Practical Approach to Spirituality
for Our Times

Deepak
Chopra

HARMONY

BOOKS · NEW YORK

Originally published in hardcover in the United States by
Harmony Books, an imprint of the Crown Publishing Group,
a division of Penguin Random House LLC, New York, in 2014.

Library of Congress Cataloging-in-Publication Data
Chopra, Deepak.
    The Future of God : a practical approach to spirituality for
our times / Deepak Chopra — First Edition.
        pages cm
1. God. 2. Religion—Philosophy. 3. Atheism—Controversial
literature. I. Title.
BL473.C465   2014
202'.11—dc23   2013008547

ISBN 978-0-307-88498-5
eBook ISBN 978-0-307-88499-2

Printed in the United States of America

Cover design by Michael Nagin

10 9 8 7 6 5 4 3 2 1

First Paperback Edition

To every seeker

Contents

THE PATH TO GOD

Stage 1: Unbelief   25

Stage 2: Faith   57

Stage 3: Knowledge   143

Prologue

aith is in trouble. For thousands of years religion has asked us to accept on faith a loving God who knows everything and possesses all power. As a result, history has walked a long and sometimes tumultuous road. There have been moments of great elation interspersed with unspeakable horrors in the name of religion. But today, in the West at least, the age of faith has drastically waned. For most people, religion is simply taken for granted. There is no living connection with God. Meanwhile, unbelief has been rising. How could it not?

Once you expose the unhealed rift between ourselves and God, a deep kind of disappointment rises to the surface. We've gone through too many catastrophes to trust in a benign, loving deity. Who can ponder the Holocaust or 9/11 and believe that God is love? Countless other heartbreaks come to mind. If you probe into what is really going on when people think about God, their comfort zone with religion shrinks. They harbor a nagging sense of doubt and insecurity.

For a long time, the burden of faith has rested on the imperfect believer. If God doesn't intervene to relieve suffering or bestow peace, the fault must be in us. In this book I've reversed things, putting the burden back on God. It is time to ask some blunt questions.

What has God done for you lately?

In supporting yourself and your family, which is more effective, having faith or working hard?

Have you ever *really* surrendered and let God solve a really tough problem for you?

Why does God allow such suffering in the world? Is this all a game or an empty promise that a loving God exists?

These questions are so troublesome that we avoid asking them, and for millions of people, they aren't even important anymore. The next technology that will improve our lives is always on the horizon. A God who matters in the twenty-first century is all but extinct.

As I see it, the real crisis in faith isn't about declining church attendance, a trend that began in Western Europe and the United States during the 1950s and continues today. The real crisis is about finding a God who matters and can be trusted. Faith presents a fork in the road, and all of us have come to it. One fork leads to a reality upheld by a living God; the other leads to a reality where God is not just absent but a fiction. In the name of this fiction, human beings have fought and died, tortured infidels, mounted bloody crusades, and performed every imaginable horror.

There's a heartrending show of cynicism in the New Testament when Jesus is on the cross—a slow and agonizing way to die—and the bystanders spit with mockery, including the chief priests of Jerusalem:

> "He saved others," they said, "but he can't save himself! He's
> the King of Israel! Let him come down now from the cross,
> and we will believe in him. He trusted God, so let God rescue
> him now if he wants him!" (Matthew 27:42–43)

The vitriol in those words hasn't diminished over time, but there's a more unsettling point. Jesus taught that people should trust in God completely, that faith can move mountains. He taught that no one should toil today or save up for tomorrow, because Providence will provide everything. Leaving aside the mystical meaning of the Crucifixion, should you and I have that kind of trust?

If people only knew it, they reach a fork in the road many times a day. I'm not writing from a Christian perspective—I practice no organized religion in my personal life—but Jesus didn't mean that Providence will supply money, food, shelter, and many other blessings if only you wait long enough. He meant this morning's food and tonight's shelter. "Ask and you will receive; knock and the door will be opened" applies to choices we make in the present moment. And this greatly raises the stakes, because if God is disappointing for all the times he hasn't come through for us, we are disappointing for all the times we have taken the road of unbelief—literally every hour of the day.

The seed of unbelief is in all of us. It offers plenty of reasons not to have faith. I hope as a compassionate human being I would have looked at the spectacle of a crucifixion and felt pity. But when it comes to my own life, I go to work, save for the future, and look over my shoulder at night on a dangerous street. I put more faith in myself than I do in an external God. I call this the zero point, the nadir of faith. At the zero point, God doesn't really matter, not when it comes down to the tough business of living. Viewed from the zero point, God is either pointless or feeble. He may look down on our suffering and feel moved, or just as likely he may greet suffering with a shrug.

For God to have a future, we must escape the zero point and find a new way of living spiritually. We don't need new religions, better scriptures, or more inspiring testimony to God's greatness. The versions we already have are good enough (and bad enough). A God worthy of faith must actually matter, and I don't see how he can until he starts to perform instead of disappoint.

Making such a radical change involves something equally radical: a total rethinking of reality. What people fail to realize is that when you challenge God, you challenge reality itself. If reality is only what appears on the surface, then there is nothing to have faith in. We can stay glued to the 24/7 news cycle and do our best to cope. Yet if reality is something that extends into higher dimensions, the story changes.

You can't rebuild a God who never existed, but you can repair a broken connection.

I decided to write a book about how to reconnect with God so that he becomes as real as a loaf of bread and as reliable as a sunrise—choose anything you trust in and know to be real. If such a God exists, there's no longer a reason to be disappointed either in him or in ourselves. Nothing like a leap of faith is required. Yet something deeper must be done, a reconsideration of what is possible. This implies an inner transformation. If someone tells you "The kingdom of heaven is within," you shouldn't think, with a twinge of guilt, *Not in me it isn't*. You should ask what it would take to make the statement true. The spiritual path begins with a curiosity that something as unbelievable as God might actually exist.

Millions of people have now heard about "the God delusion," a slogan from a band of militant atheists who are avowed enemies of faith. This disturbing movement centered around Professor Richard Dawkins cloaks its vehement, often personal attacks in terms of science and reason. Even if people don't apply the word *atheist* to themselves, many are still living as if God doesn't matter, and this affects the choices they make in their daily lives. Unbelief has implicitly won where it counts.

Faith, if it is to survive, can only be restored through a deeper exploration of the mystery of existence.

I have no harsh things to say about atheism without the militancy. Thomas Jefferson wrote, "I do not find in orthodox Christianity one redeeming feature," but he also helped found a society based on tolerance. Dawkins and company are proud to be intolerant. Atheism can be humorous about itself, as when George Bernard Shaw quipped, "Christianity might be a good thing if anyone ever tried it." Every strain of thought has its opposite, and when it comes to God, unbelief is the natural opposite of belief.

It's not right, however, to suppose that atheism is always opposed to God. According to a paradoxical 2008 Pew Research survey, 21 percent of Americans who describe themselves as atheists believe in God or a universal spirit, 12 percent believe in heaven, and 10 percent pray at least once a week. Atheists have not entirely lost faith; there's nothing in that to judge against. But Dawkins proffers spiritual nihilism with a smile and a tone of reassurance. I realized that I had to speak out against this, even though I feel no personal animus against him.

Faith must be saved for everyone's sake. From faith springs a passion for the eternal, which is even stronger than love. Many of us have lost that passion or have never known it. As I argue for God, I wish that I could instill the urgency expressed in just a few lines from Mirabai, an Indian princess who became a great mystic poet:

> *The love that binds me to you, O Lord,*
> *is unbreakable*
> *Like a diamond that smashes the hammer*
> *when it is struck.*
> *Like the lotus rising from the water*
> *my life rises from you,*
> *Like the night bird gazing at the passing moon*
> *I am lost dwelling on you.*
> *O my beloved—come back!*

In any age, faith is like this: a cry from the heart. If you are determined to believe that God doesn't exist, there's no chance that these pages will convince you that he does. The path is never closed, however. If faith can be saved, the result will be an increase in hope. By itself, faith can't deliver God, but it does something more timely: It makes God possible.

Why God Has a Future

When it comes to God, almost all of us, believers and nonbelievers alike, suffer from a kind of nearsightedness. We see—and hence believe—only what's right in front of us. The faithful see God as a benign parental figure bestowing grace and justice as he judges our actions here down below. The rest of us think God is far more distant, impersonal, and uninvolved. Yet God may be closer and more involved than that, closer than breathing, in fact.

At any given moment, someone in the world is amazed to find that the God experience is real. Wonder and certainty still dawn. I keep at hand a passage from Thoreau's *Walden* about this, where he speaks of "the solitary hired man on a farm in the outskirts of Concord, who has had his second birth." Like us, Thoreau wonders if someone's testimony about having a "peculiar religious experience" is valid. In answer, he looks across the span of centuries:

> Zoroaster, thousands of years ago, travelled the same road and had the same experience, but he, being wise, knew it to be universal.

If you find yourself suddenly infused with an experience you cannot explain, Thoreau says, just be aware that you are not alone. Your awakening is woven into the great tradition.

Humbly commune with Zoroaster then, and, through the lib-
eralizing influence of all the worthies, with Jesus Christ himself, let "our church" go by the board.

In contemporary language, Thoreau is advising us to trust our deepest
belief that spiritual experience is real. Skeptics turn this advice on its
head. The fact that God has been experienced over the ages only goes
to show that religion is a primitive holdover, a mental relic that we
should train our brains to reject. To a skeptic, God persisted in the past
because priests had the power to enforce faith, allowing no deviations
among their followers. But all attempts to clarify matters—to say, once
and for all, that God is absolutely real or absolutely unreal—continue
to fail. The muddle persists, and we all have felt the impact of confusion and doubt.

Where are you now?

Let's move from the abstract to the personal. When you look at
yourself and ask where you stand on the God issue, you are almost certainly in one of the following situations:

Unbelief: You don't accept that God is real, and you express your
   unbelief by living as if God makes no difference.
Faith: You hope that God is real, and you express your hope as
   faith.
Knowledge: You have no doubt that God is real, and therefore you
   live as if God is always present.

When someone becomes a spiritual seeker, they want to move
from unbelief to knowledge. The path is by no means clear, however.

When you get out of bed in the morning, what is the spiritual thing to do? Should you try to live in the present moment, for example, which is considered very spiritual? Peace resides in the present moment, if it resides anywhere. And yet Jesus outlines how radical such a decision actually is: "Therefore I tell you, do not worry about your life, what you will eat or what you will drink, or about your body. . . . But strive first for the kingdom of God and his righteousness, and all these things will be given to you as well. So do not worry about tomorrow, for tomorrow will bring worries of its own." (Matthew 6:25, 33–34)

In Jesus's version, living in the present implies having complete trust in God to provide everything. His confidence in God is unlimited. Whatever Jesus needs will come. But what about the poor Jewish workers who were his audience, struggling to provide the bare necessities, grimly living under the thumb of Roman oppression? They might have hoped that Providence would care for them; they might even have had enough faith to believe it. Still, surrendering was a mystical act. Only Jesus was in a state of consciousness that was totally grounded in Providence, because he saw God everywhere.

In all of us there are seeds of unbelief, because we were born in a secular age that questions everything mystical. Better to be free and skeptical than bound by myths, superstition, and dogma. When you touch the skeptic inside you, unbelief is a reasonable state to be in. But for most people it's also an unhappy state. They feel unfulfilled in a totally secular world where the deepest worship, arguably, goes to sports heroes, comic books, and having a perfect body. Science gives us no assurance that life has meaning when it describes the universe as a cold void ruled by random chance.

And so faith persists. We want the universe to be our home. We want to feel connected to creation. Above all, we don't want freedom if it means enduring perpetual anxiety and insecurity, a freedom that has lost its moorings to the meaning of life. So whether you call it clinging to faith or abiding by the traditions of our forefathers, religious belief exists everywhere. For billions of human beings there is no livable alternative.

But what about the third stage, after unbelief and faith—certain knowledge of God—which is the rarest and most elusive? To be truly certain, a person may have to undergo a transformative experience or miraculously retain the innocent soul of a young child. Neither is all that realistic in most lives. People who return from near-death experiences, which are extremely rare to begin with, have no hard evidence about "going into the light" that would convince a skeptic. What has changed for them is private, internal, and subjective. As for the innocence of children, we have good reason for abandoning it. Childhood joy is a naïve, unformed state, and as happy as it was, we yearn to experience a wider world of achievement. The creative heights of human history are reached by adults, not overgrown infants.

Let's say that you recognize yourself in one of these three states: unbelief, faith, and knowledge. It's quite all right if they are jumbled and you have passing moments of each. According to cold statistical models, most of us cluster under the middle hump of a bell-shaped curve, part of the vast majority that believes in God. At the tail end of the curve are a tiny minority: to the left, the confirmed atheists; to the right, the deeply religious who pursue God as their vocation. But it's fair to say that most people who respond that they believe in God aren't experiencing either wonder or certainty. Typically, we devote our days to everything but God: raising a family, looking for love, striving for success, reaching for more material goods on the endless conveyor belt of consumerism.

The current muddle is doing no one any good. Unbelief is haunted by inner suffering and a dread that life has no purpose. (I'm not persuaded by atheists who claim to live cheerfully in a random universe. They aren't waking up every morning to say, "How wonderful, another day when nothing really has meaning.") The state of faith is untenable in a different way: Throughout history it has led to rigidity, fanaticism, and desperate violence in the name of God. And the state of true knowledge? It seems to be the province of saints, who are exceedingly rare.

Yet God is hidden somewhere, as a shadow presence, in all three situations, whether as a negative (the deity you are fleeing when you walk away from organized religion) or as a positive (a higher reality that you aspire to). Being faintly present isn't the same as being truly important, much less the most important thing in existence. If it is possible to make God real again, I think everyone would agree to try.

This book proposes that you can move from unbelief to faith and then to true knowledge. Each is an evolutionary stage, and by exploring the first, you find that the next one opens. Evolution is voluntary when it applies to the inner world. There is complete freedom of choice. Once you know unbelief in every detail, you can remain there or move on to faith. Once you explore faith, you can do the same, accepting it as your spiritual home or looking beyond. At the end of the journey lies knowledge of God, which is just as viable—and much more real—than the first two stages. To know God isn't mystical, any more than knowing that the Earth moves around the Sun. In both cases, a fact is established, and all previous doubts and errant beliefs naturally fall away.

God Is a Verb, Not a Noun

aith has become almost impossible to enforce, especially on yourself. Our old model of God is being dismantled before our eyes.

Instead of trying to pick up the pieces, a deeper shift must take place. Reason, personal experience, and the wisdom of many cultures are coming together already. This new synthesis is like God 2.0, where human evolution takes a leap in matters of the spirit.

God 1.0 reflected human needs, which are many and varied, and these needs took on a divine personification. The needs came first. Because humans need security and safety, we projected God as our divine protector. Because life needs to be orderly, we made God the supreme lawgiver. Reversing the Book of Genesis, we created God in our own image. He did what we wanted him to do. What follows are the seven stages we fashioned for such a God.

God 1.0

Made in our image

1. **The need for safety, security, protection from harm**

   God becomes a father or mother. He controls the forces of nature, bringing good or bad fortune. Humans live like children under God's protection. His thoughts are unknowable; he acts on a whim to dispense love or punishment. Nature is orderly but is still dangerous.

This is your God if you pray for rescue, view the divine as an authority figure, believe in sin and redemption, crave miracles, and see God's hand at work when accident or disaster suddenly strikes.

2. The need to accomplish and achieve

God becomes a lawgiver. He sets down rules and follows them. This allows the future to be knowable: God will reward those who follow the law and punish those who disobey. On this foundation, human beings can build a good life and achieve material success. The secret is hard work, which pleases God, and a society that is lawful, which mirrors the laws of nature. Chaos is overcome; crime is held at bay. Nature exists to be tamed rather than feared.

This is your God if you believe that God is reasonable, wants you to succeed, rewards hard work, separates right from wrong, and has created the universe to work according to laws and principles.

3. The need to bond, to form loving families and communities

God becomes a loving presence inside every heart. The worshipper's gaze has turned inward. Bonding with others goes beyond mutual survival. Humankind is a community joined together by faith. God wants us to build a city on the hill, an ideal society. Nature exists to nourish human happiness.

This is your God if you are an idealist, optimistic about human nature, a believer in common humanity, and open to be loved by a forgiving deity. Forgiveness will be felt inside, not delivered by a priest.

4. The need to be understood

God becomes nonjudgmental. To know all is to forgive all. The wound in human nature that divides good from evil starts to heal. Tolerance increases. We develop empathy for wrongdoers, because God shows us his empathy. The need for strict reward and punishment lessens. Life has many shades of good and bad, and everything has its reasons. Nature exists to show us the full range of life in its most creative and most destructive form.

This is your God if he understands rather than judges, if you see yourself sympathetically because God does, if you accept good and evil as inevitable aspects of creation, if God tells you that you are understood.

5.   The need to create, discover, and explore

God becomes a creative source. He gave us our birthright of curiosity. He remains unknowable, but he unfolds one secret after another in creation. At the far edge of the universe, the unknown is a challenge and a source of wonder. God wants us not to worship but to evolve. Our role is to discover and explore. Nature exists to provide endless mysteries that challenge our intelligence—there is always more to discover.

This is your God if you live to explore and be creative, if you feel happiest confronting the unknown, if you have total confidence that nature can be unraveled, including human nature, as long as we keep questioning and never settle for fixed, preordained truth.

6.   The need for moral guidance and inspiration

God becomes pure wonder. After reason has reached the limits of understanding, the mystery remains. Sages, saints, and the divinely inspired have penetrated it. They have felt a divine presence that transcends everyday life. Materialism is an illusion. Creation was fashioned in two layers, the visible and the invisible. Miracles become real when everything is a miracle. To reach God, one must accept the reality of invisible things. Nature is a mask for the divine.

This is your God if you are a spiritual seeker. You want to know what lies behind the mask of materialism, to find the source of healing, to experience peace, and to be in direct contact with a divine presence.

7. Unity, the state beyond all needs

God becomes One. There is complete fulfillment because you have reached the goal of seeking. You experience the divine everywhere. The last hint of separation has vanished. You have no need to divide saint from sinner, because God imbues everything. In this state, you don't know the truth; you become it. The universe and every event in it are expressions of a single underlying Being, which is pure awareness, pure intelligence, and pure creativity. Nature is the outward form that consciousness takes as it unfolds in time and space.

This is your God if you feel totally connected to your soul and your source. Your consciousness has expanded to embrace a cosmic perspective. You see everything happening in the mind of God. The ecstasy of great mystics, who seem especially gifted or chosen, now becomes available to you, because you have fully matured spiritually.

The God that brings the scheme to an end, God as One, is different from the others. He isn't a projection. He signifies a state of total certainty and wonder, and if you can reach that state, you are no longer projecting. Every need has been fulfilled; the path has ended with reality itself.

Looking at the list, you may not identify with any need that God might fulfill. That's understandable when belief is a muddle. No version of God is strong enough to win your allegiance. The muddle is also rooted in how the brain processes choices. When you are deciding in a restaurant whether to order a salad or a greasy cheeseburger, separate groups of neurons in the cerebral cortex organize your choice. One group promotes ordering a salad, the other promotes having a cheeseburger. You are making up your mind.

But at the same time, each neuronal group sends out chemical signals to suppress the activity of the other. This phenomenon, known as "cross-inhibition," is being newly studied by brain researchers. The basic notion is a familiar one: In sports, the fans root for their team and boo the other team. In every armed conflict, soldiers are told that God is on their side but not the other. Us-versus-them thinking probably has a deep brain connection. Referring to spiritual doubts, the idea of a loving Father cross-inhibits the idea of a punishing Father. Each one has its rationale, and each diminishes the other. A loving father should love all his children equally, yet every people favored by God have suffered without cause. God's behavior is as erratic as our own, so that any reason to worship one kind of God is inhibited by a competing version—seven competing versions, in fact.

If God 1.0 is a projection, does that mean God doesn't exist? Has another nail been driven into his coffin? Not necessarily. The fact that Richard Dawkins and company reject God doesn't mean that their view is complete or true. Ask a teenager to describe his parents, and you'll get an unreliable description. As an adolescent, he has a muddled view of what parents are like. It mixes a child's need for love, security, and protection with an adult's need for independence, self-reliance, and selfhood. When the two sides meet, they cross-inhibit each other. No one would take a teenager's criticism of his parents at full faith, much less abolish the institution of the family based on it. Likewise, in our muddled view of God, we are unreliable witnesses to the true nature of the divine, and our doubts don't mean that God should be abolished.

A New Version, God 2.0

Every age creates a God that serves only for a while (although that while can be centuries). Our age makes the most minimal demand on spirit: We want a deity that we can freely ignore.

How, then, should we re-create God? I'm speaking of God in the West. Other varieties of God are not ready for renewal. Fundamentalist Islam is a rearguard action that is desperately trying to preserve God 1.0, insisting on the most primitive version, a God who protects the faithful from annihilation; such a God cannot help but be a matter of life and death. Nor am I speaking of God in the East, which has a long tradition of seeing God as One. That's God 1.0 in the seventh stage, a presence that imbues all of creation. Such a deity has no location except at the source of our consciousness, which can only be found after an inner journey. God as the higher self is the ultimate revelation. Countless people in Asia are brought up to believe in the higher self—in India it is called Atman—but they don't actually undertake the inner journey. As in the West, most people in the East live as if God were optional, a fixture of their cultural heritage that makes little or no difference in how their practical life turns out.

In order to have a future, God must fulfill the promises made in his name throughout history. Instead of being a projection, God 2.0 is the reverse. He is the reality from which existence springs. As you journey inward, everyday life becomes suffused with divine qualities like love, forgiveness, and compassion. These are experienced in yourself as a reality. God 2.0 does much more—he is the interface between you and infinite consciousness. As things are now, a God experience is rare, barely hinted at, because our focus is on the outer world and material goals. When you begin the process of finding God, the inner world reveals itself. God experience will start to become the norm, not in a spectacular way like a wished-for miracle but in the far deeper way of transformation.

God 2.0

Making the Connection

First connection: God experience dawns

You become centered. The mind calms down and gains more self-awareness. Restlessness and dissatisfaction decrease. You have moments of bliss and inner peace, which become more frequent. You find less resistance in your life. You feel that you matter in the larger scheme of things. Everyday life gets easier. You feel less stress, struggle, and pressure.

Deeper connection: God experience transforms you

Higher consciousness becomes real. You appreciate the value of simply being. Your desires come true with much less effort than before. In bursts of insight, you see why you exist and what your purpose is. Outer distractions lose their grip on you. You feel emotionally bonded with those you love. Anxiety and struggle drastically decrease. Your life is pervaded with a sense of rightness.

Total connection: Your true self is God

You merge with your source. God is revealed as pure consciousness, the essence of who you are. In time, this essence will radiate in all of creation. You experience the light of life within yourself. All is forgiven; all is loved. Your individual ego has expanded to become the cosmic ego. As enlightenment deepens, you experience a second birth. From now on, your evolution will take place as a journey into the transcendent.

In reality you are completely connected to God already, since we are talking about the source of existence. But there are different states of consciousness, and reality changes in each of them. If your awareness is turned outward, focused on the material world with its precarious ups and downs, you will perceive no God. The outer world will be sufficient on its own terms. If instead you look beyond external appearances, focusing on higher values such as love and understanding, your faith in God offers security and reassurance. But only when you transform your own awareness will God become clear, real, and useful. Until then, the divine has a shadow reality and is almost useless. The skeptics are right to question such a God. Their mistake is that they are blind to a better one.

In a word, God 2.0 is a process, a verb instead of a noun. Once you begin the process, it builds upon itself. You will know that you are on the right path because each step brings insight, clarity, and expanded experiences—they validate that higher consciousness is real.

When there is enough consciousness, God appears. You will know this as surely as you know that you have thoughts, feelings, and sensations. *This is God* will cross your mind as easily as *This is a rose*. The presence of God will be as palpable as a heartbeat.

Three states of awareness

That's what lies ahead. We have to give equal weight to the three states that people find themselves in right now, since unbelief, faith, and knowledge all serve a purpose. They are the stepping-stones from "No God" to "Perhaps God" to "God in me."

Unbelief: In this stage a person is guided by reason and doubt. The "No God" position feels reasonable. It is arrived at by questioning all of God's inconsistencies and the myths surrounding religion. Science plays its part, not by proving or disproving God but by showing us how to ask skeptical questions. Unbelief isn't just negation: There is positive atheism, too, the kind that focuses on God as a possibility but refuses to accept tradition, dogma, or faith without evidence. This strain of unbelief leads to mental clarity. It forces us to grow up and act like adults, spiritually speaking, defying the pull of inertia that makes it all too easy to accept the God of Sunday school lessons.

Imagine that your brain has neural pathways dedicated to unbelief. These pathways process the world as it comes to you through your five senses. It trusts in objects it can see and touch. It distrusts anything mystical. Rocks are hard, knives are sharp, but God is intangible. A good deal of yourself is attached to this area of the brain, which spans diverse regions. The primitive drives of hunger, fear, anger, sex, and self-defense throw you into the physical world, here and now. Life consists of gratifying your desires in the present, not postponing them until you arrive in heaven. At the same time, unbelief incorporates the higher brain function of reason and discrimination, as well as the entire project (which has no definite location in the brain) of building a strong ego, an "I" that is never satisfied for long. All of this neural processing works against the reality of God. It will do no good to pretend. Life is a demanding taskmaster, and God has failed to make it any different.

Faith: Even as modern life has eroded every organized religion, people still identify with faith. In polls, 75 percent of Americans identify themselves with an organized religion, whatever their doubts may be. To a skeptic, clinging to faith seems childish and weak. At worst it's a primitive defense that shields a person who is unable to handle reality. But for the process of restoring God, faith is crucial. It gives you a goal and a vision. It tells you where you are headed long before you arrive. (I like a metaphor I once heard, that faith is like smelling the sea before you see it.)

Faith can be negative. We all know the perils of faith-based fanaticism. The step from believing in the promise of heavenly rewards to becoming a suicide bomber is frighteningly small. Beyond the ranks of fanatics, faith demands its price. The "good" Catholic and "good" Jew are proud not to think for themselves. Faith supports a deeply conservative impulse, and when we are honest with ourselves, we all wish for the security and belonging in which tradition enfolds the faithful.

In the functioning brain, faith spans its own neural networks. A major part of the activity takes place in the limbic system, the seat of emotions. Faith is attached to love of family and devotion to your parents when you were a child. Memory invokes nostalgia for a better time and place; faith tells you that you will get there once more. But your higher brain is also involved. Throughout religious history the faithful have suffered persecution. Turning the other cheek instead of lashing back in revenge requires the higher brain to hold on to evolved values like compassion, forgiveness, and detachment. We all know what it feels like to have forgiveness and retaliation conflicting inside us; it's a classic example of cross-inhibition in the brain.

Knowledge: The only way to end inner conflict is to arrive at a state of certainty. The trail leads from "I have faith that God exists" to "I know God exists." You can drum skepticism into children from a young age (there is actually a Web site devoted to showing kids how to "escape" from God); you can fool believers into following a false messiah. Knowledge is different when it comes from inside. You know that you exist; you know that you are conscious. God 2.0 needs nothing else as a foundation. The expansion of consciousness brings true spiritual knowledge completely on its own.

God isn't like Halley's comet—you can't wait for him to appear in the sky. You can't think your way to God, either. Fortunately, you don't have to. You begin by seeking, and your search builds upon itself. God isn't like the dinosaurs. One *T. rex* fossil suffices to settle the question of whether dinosaurs once roamed the earth. Knowing God consists of many experiences acquired over a lifetime, a slow-motion epiphany, as it were. Certainly you will experience temporary peaks, striking revelations and moments when the truth seems astonishingly clear. A selected few may be blinded by the light of God on the road to Damascus. For them, God is revealed in a flash.

But the brain tells a different story. Healthy brain function depends on reliable neural pathways that work the same every time. If you've trained yourself to play the piano or throw a football, the skill became dependable because you laid down specific neural pathways. Every experience either adds to your skill or subtracts from it. Although you don't realize it, your brain is always building new pathways and diverting or even destroying other ones. At the microscopic level where neuron meets neuron, God needs his own pathways.

In a slow-motion epiphany, you train your brain to adapt to spiritual experiences. According to a popular notion, any of us can master a

skill if we devote ten thousand hours to it: playing the violin, perform-
ing close-up magic, developing super memory, or any other goal. This
theory has a basic validity, because altering old pathways and building
new ones takes time and repetition. God 2.0 is more than a project in
brain remodeling, but unless your brain is remodeled, the experience of
God will be impossible. An adage from the Vedic tradition in India says,
"This isn't knowledge you learn. It is knowledge you become." Viewed
through the lens of neuroscience, that's literally true.

The God process incorporates the whole person. I invite you to
disbelieve anything you've ever heard about God, and I invite you to
keep the faith at the same time. If God is One, you should leave nothing
out, including the most extreme skepticism. Reality isn't fragile. If you
doubt a rose, it doesn't wither and die. The only prerequisite is that you
accept the possibility that God 2.0 could be real.

A famous guru was once asked, "How should I be your disciple?
Should I worship you? Should I accept every word as truth?" The guru
replied, "Neither one. Just open your mind to the possibility that what
I'm saying could be true." Suppressing any inner potential—including
the potential to find God—aborts it. The seed is killed before it sprouts.
Having an open mind is like opening a shuttered window. The light
will enter of its own accord.

think it's clear that we're not talking about a come-to-Jesus moment.
Self-transformation is more like child development. When you were
four years old playing with paper dolls and watching *Sesame Street,* your
brain was still developing; in the course of time you abandoned paper
dolls and began reading books. There was no single moment where the
road forked, where you had to choose to be four or five, six or seven.
You were simply yourself, while at an invisible level evolution was
exerting its force.

The process of self-transformation works the same way. You remain yourself while invisible changes take place deep inside. Every per-

son is like a ragged army. Some aspects of your personality scout ahead, while the camp followers lag behind. The spiritual path feels as if you are flying ahead one day and foot-dragging, or even backsliding, the next. Unbelief, faith, and knowledge all have their say.

But eventually, if you remain self-aware and keep track of the process, you will make real progress. There will be more days when you feel safe and protected, and fewer days when you feel alone and lost. Moments of bliss will increase. Feeling secure in your inner core becomes a baseline feeling. The self is like a hologram, where any small piece can stand for the whole. The process that builds the God experience scrambles the old hologram, splinter by splinter. You will see a new wholeness when the job is done. That wholeness is God.

THE PATH TO GOD

Stage 1: Unbelief

Dawkins and His Delusions

Unbelief isn't the born enemy of faith. In modern times, in fact, unbelief is a reasonable starting point. But it's a poor end point. The most virulent protests against God can be used to clear the mind of false beliefs, paving the way for stronger faith. In that way Richard Dawkins, an avowed enemy of God, becomes God's tacit ally.

When *The God Delusion* appeared in 2006 and became a major bestseller, Dawkins gave militant atheism its polemical stance. Dawkins does not just reject God; he shows contempt for spirituality altogether. He mocks our aspirations to connect with a higher reality, basing his argument on the most simplistic grounds: that the physical world is all there is. He portrays religion as a deluded state, with no basis in reality.

There is no denying the power of *The God Delusion* when it indicts religion in its most fanatical forms. At one point, Dawkins co-opts John Lennon's gentle song "Imagine" and turns it to his own purposes.

Imagine, with John Lennon, a world with no religion. Imagine no suicide bombers, no 9/11, no 7/7, no Crusades, no witch-hunts, no Gunpowder Plot, no Indian partition, no Israeli/Palestinian wars, no Serb/Croat/Muslim massacres, no persecution of Jews as "Christ killers," no Northern Ireland "troubles," no "honor killings," no shiny-suited, bouffant-haired televangelists fleecing gullible people of their money ("God wants you to give until it hurts").

As the horrific examples pile up, Dawkins's confidence builds; he isn't offering hope or sympathy here. He's venting his contempt.

> Imagine no Taliban to blow up ancient statues, no public beheadings of blasphemers, no flogging of female skin for the crime of showing an inch of it.

You would think, after hearing this litany of horrors, that converts would flock to join the atheist cause, but they haven't. The decline of organized religion in America, along with Western Europe, began in the 1950s and hasn't reversed. The unchecked catastrophes of the twentieth century emptied the pews at a steady pace. But there hasn't been a mass embrace of Dawkins-style unbelief, which cannot abide God and must attack anyone who is a believer. Why have people deserted religion without deserting God? This is an important question that Dawkins remains blind to.

Let's go back to when *Time* magazine ran a cover story in 1966 asking the question "Is God Dead?" A rift was opened, in which people dared to ask the question, once unthinkable, and in the four decades since, the rift has only grown wider. Dawkins threw a bomb into the rift. (*Time* put him on the cover for his efforts in 2007.) He called the God of the Old Testament an "appalling role model" in no uncertain terms—Jehovah is "the most unpleasant character in all fiction: jealous and proud of it; a petty, unjust, unforgiving control freak; a vindictive, bloodthirsty ethnic cleanser; a misogynist, pestilential, megalomaniacal, sadomasochistic, capriciously malevolent bully." A Godless world, Dawkins claimed, would be better in every way.

Moving on to the New Testament, Dawkins wrote, "The historical evidence that Jesus claimed any sort of divine status is minimal." If such evidence ever emerged, then the evidence would indicate that Jesus might have been mad; at best he was "honestly mistaken." The only plausible reason that religion ever took hold, Dawkins tells us, is that our ancestors heard fairy tales and, like "gullible children," believed they were true. Being duped was good enough for primitive brains, but we need to grow up. If Dawkins can convince us once and for all that God is a worthless holdover from the age of superstition, the Holy Ghost won't stand a ghost of a chance.

Dawkins prides himself on being the absolute atheist, capable of pulling stunts like the one involving the visit of Pope Benedict XVI to the U.K. in the fall of 2010. It was the first official state visit to Great Britain by any pontiff and was deemed controversial on a number of grounds, including the Church's position on contraception and the ongoing scandal of sexual abuse among the priesthood. Dawkins's participation in a "Protest the Pope" rally was far more extreme. No accusation was too inflammatory or reckless. He had previously backed the notion that a warrant should be issued for the pope's arrest for "crimes against humanity." At the rally Dawkins gave a speech that brought up Benedict's association with Hitler Youth in the 1930s, not mentioning that this was required of all German youths at the time—the pope's father actually spoke out against Hitler. Dawkins accused the Church of supporting Nazism, called Hitler a Roman Catholic (the dictator was born into a Catholic family but stopped practicing the faith after childhood), and repeated the denunciation that the pope was "an enemy of humanity."

Anti-Catholicism in this virulent vein—a prominent Catholic newspaper editor called the attack "lunatic"—has never been acceptable in civilized society. It fosters discord and religious prejudice. Dawkins had already become a public celebrity for *The God Delusion,* and his academic prestige masked attitudes that would have been found disgraceful in an ordinary citizen—and that should have disgraced him. He wrongly appropriated the authority of being a professor and biologist at Oxford University. In his own field, Dawkins's previous writings on evolution and genes had made him perhaps the most respected explainer of science in his generation—his official Oxford title is not about any specific field of scientific expertise and has nothing to do with research; he is Simonyi Professor for the Public Understanding of Science. Moving on to the public misunderstanding of God was a perverse step.

The God Delusion is aimed at a specific target audience, the author tells us: all the doubters who remain in the religion of their parents but don't believe in it anymore, and who worry about the evils done in the name of God. A multitude of people want to flee from religion, he writes, but they "don't realize that leaving is an option." The motto for *The God Delusion,* in fact, is "I didn't know I could." Dawkins believes that he is advancing the human spirit; he presents himself as a freedom fighter. As he declares on the very first page, "Being an atheist is nothing to be apologetic about. On the contrary, it is something to be proud of, standing tall to face the far horizon."

The God Delusion received some scathing reviews for its extremist tactics. There is more to religion than the terrible acts committed by fanatics, but not in Dawkins's argument, where he explicitly says that moderate religion should be condemned equally with the most intolerant fundamentalism. (One chapter is titled "How 'Moderation' in Faith Fosters Fanaticism.") Militant atheism equates absolutism with certainty. Once branded as "very evil," believing in God makes a saint as guilty as Osama bin Laden.

The multitudes of doubters just waiting to be liberated by the message of *The God Delusion* don't exist. They are Dawkins's delusion.

None of his flaws, mistakes, and shifty tactics are difficult to spot. But many readers gave *The God Delusion* a free pass, I think. It proclaims to uphold rationality over irrationality; it flatters secular society for being superior to religious society. But I suspect that the major reason is psychological. Dawkins is telling troubled doubters that they have no reason to be guilty, confused, lost, or lonely. They are on the cusp of a new world that is brighter and better than anything to be offered by spirituality. He offers atheism as comfort and reassurance—which it may be for some.

But if the possibility of God is so backward that any rational mind would reject it, why did Einstein devote a considerable amount of time trying to fit God into the new universe he pioneered? It's a question worth pursuing, because the stark contrast between reason and unreason dominates *The God Delusion* on every page. If the twentieth century's greatest mind didn't accept that science is the enemy of religion, he might have seen deeper than Dawkins. Which guide to the future should we trust, after all?

Einstein's spirituality

Einstein wasn't a conventional believer, but he was compassionate enough to realize that loss of faith can be devastating, all the more if God has been central in your life. At first his story conforms to that of many twentieth-century skeptics. As a young man, he rejected religion and his own Judaism on logical grounds, unable to accept the literal truth of events recounted in the Old Testament. Creation in seven days, God speaking to Moses from a burning bush, Jacob wrestling with the angel: Many turn-of-the-century Jews couldn't reasonably support the miracle world of ancient Judaism. (Later in life Einstein said, "The idea of a personal God is alien to me and seems even naïve.") Einstein moved beyond orthodox faith while still struggling personally with his Jewishness. He could have followed the easy trajectory of a Dawkins, using science as a weapon to combat the vestiges of faith. *The God Delusion* has a short section on Einstein, gathering him into the fold as an "atheist scientist." Certainly Einstein wasn't a mystic. But Dawkins discounts a personal journey that actually points where spirituality is headed, even today.

Einstein was interested in the essence of religion, which he thought was completely genuine. An anecdote stands out in Walter Isaacson's recent biography. At a dinner party in Berlin in 1929, where Einstein was in attendance, the conversation turned to astrology, which the guests dismissed as superstitious and unbelievable. When someone said that God fell into the same category, the host tried to silence him, pointing out that even Einstein believed in God. "That isn't possible!" the guest exclaimed. In reply, Einstein gave one of his subtlest and most consistent reasons for believing:

"Try and penetrate with our limited means the secrets of nature, and you will find that, behind all the discernible laws and connections, there remains something subtle, intangible, and inexplicable. Veneration for this force beyond anything we can comprehend is my religion. To that extent I am, in fact, religious."

This comment is rich with possibilities. It reinforces the idea that a modern search for God shouldn't be pursuing the old image of a patriarch sitting on his throne. Einstein wasn't after that. He was looking for God behind the curtain of material appearances. The key here is *subtlety*. Like all scientists, Einstein explored the material world, but he perceived a subtler region of existence. Notice that he didn't claim that his religious belief was based on faith. Perception was involved, and discovery through the mind.

Einstein took the bolder step of trying to understand whether a single reality encompasses both the drive to believe in a higher reality and the drive to explain nature in terms of laws and processes that operate independently of spirit. Time, space, and gravity don't need God, yet without God the universe seems random and meaningless. Einstein expressed this dichotomy in his famous saying: "Science without religion is lame. Religion without science is blind."

Another of his famous quotes touches on the mind again: "The religious inclination lies in the dim consciousness that dwells in humans that all nature, including the humans in it, is in no way an accidental game, but a work of lawfulness, that there is a fundamental cause of all existence." The main thought here is about the orderliness of nature. Einstein could not believe that the kind of intricate beauty that surrounds us was accidental. He fought his whole life against the random universe explained by quantum mechanics. Without really understanding what he meant, the public was on Einstein's side when he said that God doesn't play dice with the universe.

But what stands out for me in this quote is a passing phrase: "all nature, including the humans in it." Lesser scientists, including the popular skeptics like Dawkins, make the mistake of believing that humans can stand outside nature and look into its workings like children pressing their noses against a bakery shop window. They presume objectivity of the kind that quantum physics totally abolished almost a hundred years ago. The observer plays an active part in what he observes. We live in a participatory universe.

Beyond a purely scientific argument, Einstein understood the ambiguity of the human situation. Our "dim consciousness" of something beyond the observable universe puts us in a strange position. Which should we trust, consciousness or objective facts? Science itself was born in "dim consciousness," if you think about it. Instead of accepting the world of sight, sound, touch, taste, and smell, the scientific mind transcends appearances. It thinks, "Perhaps there are invisible laws at work here. God's creation may obey these laws. He might even want his children to discover them, as part of their reverence for Creation."

We need to remember that Copernicus, Kepler, and Galileo had to wrestle with the age of faith personally; they were men of that age as well as pioneers of a new age. Religion defined how everyone participated in the universe. The first rule was that God transcends the visible world. It took inner struggle to switch this over and say that mathematics transcends the visible world, because once you elevate mathematics, you elevate the laws of nature that operate according to mathematics. It's a slippery slope. Suddenly undreamed-of thoughts enter your head. Perhaps God is subject to the same laws. He can't overturn gravity. Or is God just playing at being powerless? Having decided to let Creation run mechanically, as if ruled by mathematical precision, he could topple the whole machine if he wanted to.

Einstein's search moved in much the same shadowy world. He couldn't explain what lay beyond time and space—he had pushed the mathematics of time and space as far as it could go—but he didn't make the crude mistake of dismissing his "dim consciousness" of higher reality as a throwback to superstition. This kind of ambiguity frustrated many people at the time. Dawkins is right to point out in *The God Delusion* that believers and atheists both like to cherry-pick Einstein's contradictory statements about God. They want the greatest thinker in the world to give definitive answers.

A prominent rabbi sent Einstein an exasperated telegram: "Do you believe in God? Stop. Answer paid. Fifty words." Einstein replied, "I believe in Spinoza's God, who reveals himself in the lawful harmony of all that exists, but not in a God who concerns himself with the fate and the doings of mankind." Influenced by the freethinking Dutch philosopher Spinoza, he became fascinated by the possibility that matter and mind form one reality, and that God is the supreme intelligence suffusing that reality. He praised Spinoza as "the first philosopher to deal with the soul and body as one, and not two separate things."

By middle age, Einstein had rejected a personal God, putting himself beyond the confines of the Judeo-Christian tradition. But not entirely: When he was fifty, an interviewer asked Einstein if he had been influenced by Christianity, to which he replied, "I am a Jew, but I am enthralled by the luminous figure of the Nazarene." Clearly surprised, the interviewer asked if Einstein believed that Jesus had actually existed. "Unquestionably. No one can read the Gospels without feeling the actual presence of Jesus. His personality pulsates in every word. No myth is filled with such life."

Even so, Einstein was progressing personally toward a spirituality far more secular than this comment suggests. Secular spirituality looks at the wholeness of existence without prejudice. God and reason are allowed to coexist without fighting. How? The link is at the level of mind. Einstein's ultimate goal, he said, was to understand God's mind. But to do that, the human mind must be explained first. After all, our minds are the filter through which we perceive reality, and if this filter is distorted and misunderstood, we have no possibility of grasping God's mind. Either we think like him or he thinks like us. If neither is true, there can be no connection.

Einstein surpasses Dawkins in every way as a guide to both religion and science. Without a shadow of arrogance, Einstein wrote, "What separates me from most so-called atheists is a feeling of utter humility toward the unattainable secrets of the harmony of the cosmos." (*The God Delusion* relates nothing about Einstein's actual spiritual journey, in keeping with Dawkins's loose relation to the truth.) For me, the most inspiring trait is Einstein's fascination with a level of creation just out of reach. It's the unseen place where wonder begins. In his 1930 credo, "What I Believe," we find this sentence: "To sense that behind anything that can be experienced there is something that our minds cannot grasp, whose beauty and sublimity reaches us only indirectly, this is religiousness." Statements like these open the way for a broad, tolerant view of the spiritual quest. In that regard, Einstein outshines the rigidity of current scientific skeptics, who throw out a personal God but leave a vacuous sterility in his place.

Answering Militant Atheism

Richard Dawkins, espousing atheism-as-progress, has been joined by other prominent voices. They include three best-selling writers: the philosopher Daniel Dennett, the late polemicist Christopher Hitchens, and the anti-Christian lightning rod, former student of Buddhism, and neuroscientist Sam Harris. The books they write are deliberate provocations, but I am puzzled by how shallow their arguments against God actually are. They gleefully distort spirituality and have no qualms about using unfair tactics. Hitchens, for example, throws out spiritual testimony before it even has its say.

> Any decent intellectual argument has to begin by excluding people who claim to know more than they can possibly know. You start off by saying, "Well, that's wrong to begin with. Now can we get on with it?" So theism is gone in the first round. It's off the island. It's out of the show.

Personally, I can't imagine a better formula for intellectual dishonesty. The spokesmen for militant atheism don't confront their own tunnel vision; they revel in it instead. All ideologues do. This leads them into making blind misstatements. Here's a sampling taken from taped talks:

> Harris: "Every religious person feels the same criticism of other people's faiths that we do as atheists. They reject

the pseudo-miracles . . . they see the confidence tricks in other people's faith."

Hitchens: Religious people "like the idea that [God] can't be demonstrated, because then there would be nothing to be faithful about. If everyone had seen the Resurrection and we all knew we'd been saved by it, then we would be living in an unalterable system of belief—it would have to be policed."

Harris again: "If the Bible is not a magic book, Christianity evaporates. If the Koran is not a magic book, Islam evaporates. If you look at these books, is there . . . a single sentence that could not have been uttered by a person for whom a wheelbarrow would have been emergent technology?"

Raw prejudice is spewed out all over the place, yet in a skeptical age, militant atheism has gotten a good deal of intellectual respect. Dennett, who argues that we are all "zombies" mechanically following the dictates of our brains, is widely praised for debunking such worn-out notions as the soul and the personal self. Hitchens's provocative book, *god is not Great* (lowercasing *God* is his choice, in the title and throughout the text), was a finalist for the National Book Award. In 2011, during his last dying days, as he succumbed to cancer of the esophagus—the sad outcome of being a lifelong heavy drinker and smoker—Hitchens wrote an open letter to an annual atheist convention in America.

His message was poignant in its defiance of any death-bed conversion. Here are a few excerpts.

I have found, as the enemy [death] becomes more familiar, that all the special pleading for salvation, redemption and supernatural deliverance appears even more hollow . . . than it did before.

I have found my trust better placed in two things: the skill and principle of advanced medical science and the comradeship of innumerable friends and family, all of them immune to the false consolations of religion.

It is these forces among others which will speed the day when humanity emancipates itself from the mind-forged manacles of servility and superstition.

The key terms that Hitchens uses in his letter to condemn an old, discredited worldview are familiar in the rhetoric of militant atheism: "superstition," "false consolation," "mind-forged manacles of servility," "stultifying pseudo-science," and the "blandishments" of organized religion. Against these inimical forces he amasses the impulse for good that is on his side: decency, skepticism, "our innate solidarity," courage, "sincere resistance to insidious nonsense," and so on.

Rhetoric is just rhetoric, and few take seriously that atheists are models of decency and morality while all believers are servile and superstitious. Human nature is not so neatly parceled out. At the emotional level I am most disturbed by bullying behavior that seeks to crush the early shoots of personal spirituality. In my experience, people who have left the reassurance of traditional faiths usually feel insecure. Their spiritual yearning is vague and unformed. They aren't armed against the arguments of militant atheists. Dawkins, Hitchens, Harris, and Dennett are professional writers and thinkers; they have mastered the art of persuasion. They are unashamed to marshal dishonest arguments just for the sake of winning, or out of disdain for their opponents. In a flash, Dawkins and his cohorts lump anyone who utters the word "God" in with the crudest religious fundamentalism. There are many shades of atheism also. It's worth repeating that 2008 Pew survey I began with, which found that 21 percent of American who describe themselves as atheists believe in God or a universal spirit. The same poll found that 12 percent of atheists believe in heaven, and 10 percent pray at least once a week.

What about the claim that we would all enjoy life more if we dropped the preposterous notion that God exists? The Irish-American writer T. C. Boyle gave the lie to this in a doleful remark made in an interview with the *New York Times*. The topic of death came up—Boyle's novels feature death prominently—and his telling response goes to the heart of what disillusionment actually feels like.

> In previous generations, there was purpose; you had to die, but there was God, and literature and culture would go on. Now, of course, there is no God, and our species is imminently doomed, so there is no purpose. We get up, raise families, have bank accounts, fix our teeth and everything else. But really, there is utterly no purpose except to be alive.

For many, this kind of disillusionment feels very real, but no one would call it a happy state of mind. Leave out the tainted word *God* with all its bad connotations. Substitute a synonym for what seekers want, such as *inner peace, spiritual fulfillment, the soul, higher consciousness, the transcendent*. Wiping them off the face of the earth isn't the key to a happier existence. It's more like a preview of hell on earth. The happiness that is supposed to follow when you give up on your spiritual aspirations is hollow.

None of this is hard to see. But it is hard to counter, because militant atheism makes the right diagnosis while offering the wrong medicine. The right medicine is spiritual renewal. We are essentially spiritual beings. Our place in creation isn't defined by being intelligent—

although we are proud of that—but by aspiring to reach higher. Militant atheism would crush this precious trait. It would exchange the tragedy of a failed God for the tragedy of having no soul. Science and the data it collects contain no wonder, awe, or mystery. The joy of existence has no reality except inside us—we add the wonder, and we can take it away.

Christopher Hitchens died of cancer ten days before Christmas 2011. He was sixty-two. The kind of existential courage he showed, in the "long argument I am currently having with the specter of death," is honorable and touching. It is equally honorable to be a spiritual seeker, and ironically, there's a convergence here. Spirituality is existential, too. It asks who we are, why we are here, and what the highest values are by which a person should live.

The atheist's mistake is to hog the moral limelight, declaring that only nonbelievers own the truth. The truth is a process of discovery, and someone who scorns the process needs to wake up before claiming that anyone else is fast asleep. When they talk to pollsters, people almost unanimously express a belief in God. But the seed of unbelief hasn't been plucked out. To begin the process of rebooting God, each of us needs to hold up a mirror to our own unbelief. That may seem like a frightening or disheartening prospect. It isn't. When you remove the illusions that you trust in, what remains is the truth, and the ultimate truth is God.

Proving the Platypus

God's existence is hard to prove, but so is one of nature's most whimsical creations, the platypus. If it didn't really exist, no one would give much credence to this improbable creature. It has webbed feet and a bill like a duck. The male can deliver a venomous sting with his hind feet. The female doesn't give birth like other mammals but lays eggs like a fish, reptile, or bird. Let's say that a mathematician is called in to prove how unlikely such a creature is. With enough reliable variables, he could give you a statistical probability, and it would be very low. A fishlike, reptilian mammal defies all the odds. Yet lo and behold, those odds prove to be wrong as soon as a platypus is dug out of its burrow beside an Australian stream. (They are shy, nocturnal creatures.)

Beware of arguments based on probability. When he was a young man, Einstein worked as a clerk in the Swiss Patent Office. What are the odds that a clerk in the same office today will be the next Einstein? It's an absurd question to pose that way (like asking the odds that a deaf person will become the next Beethoven). Even if you came up with plausible odds (ten zillion to one), the next Einstein won't be found using probability. Likewise, when you want to get on a bus, you don't calculate the probability of its taking you where you want to go. You consult the schedule and find out. There are lots of wrong questions that lead to wrong answers.

In *The God Delusion*, Dawkins makes improbability the centerpiece of denying God's existence. It's a classic case of asking the wrong question. His argument can be found in a chapter titled "Why There Almost Certainly Is No God," which poses as objectivity. On a scale of 1 to 7, where 1 is certainty that God exists and 7 is certainty that he doesn't, he counts himself a 6: "I cannot know for certain, but I think God is very improbable, and I live my life on the assumption that he is not there."

Why should the existence of God come down to calculating the odds like a horse race? You don't need to call in a statistician if you've found a platypus, and for three thousand years the same has held true of God. People have had many direct experiences of God throughout history. Writing in the generation after the Crucifixion, Saint Paul declared that more than five hundred converts had seen the risen Christ. Muhammad went up to a cave above Mecca where he found peace and quiet, only to be confronted by the angel Gabriel, who commanded him to "Recite!" Spontaneously Muhammad began to speak the verses of the Koran. Religious history is filled with epiphanies, revelations, visions, miracles, and wonders. With a phenomenon as universal as spirituality, direct experience means something. A skeptic has a right to discount something generic like a public opinion poll. The fact that 80 to 90 percent of Americans believe in God is weak evidence unless you interview each respondent and ask them why they believe.

God (unlike the platypus) may be invisible, but so is music. We trust our experience of music, but what if a deaf skeptic came along? How would you prove the existence of music to him? You could take him to concert halls where people have gathered to enjoy music. If he remained unconvinced, you'd have many other options: music conservatories, factories where musical instruments are made, and so on. At a certain point, even if a deaf skeptic had no ability to validate that music is real, the vast experience of others would be convincing—unless he was dead set against it.

Dawkins is dead set against acknowledging the existence of God; therefore the direct experience of other people carries no weight with him. All are deluded and duped. *The God Delusion* has a detailed index at the back. Here are some names that do not appear in it: Buddha, Lao-tzu, Zoroaster, Socrates, Plato, Saint Francis of Assisi, and the gospel writers Matthew, Mark, Luke, and John. Dawkins dismisses all spiritual experience from the past with a shrug. He doesn't mention Confucius, either, and his single reference to Confucianism gets lumped in with Buddhism because to Dawkins they aren't really spiritual in nature:

> I shall not be concerned at all with other religions such as Buddhism or Confucianism. Indeed, there is something to be said for treating these not as religions but as ethical systems or philosophies of life.

This will come as news to many generations of Buddhist priests and Tibetan lamas. But then, Dawkins is the kind of writer who wants the reader to accept that Judaism was "originally a tribal cult of a single fierce, unpleasant God, morbidly obsessed with sexual restrictions, with the smell of charred flesh," and so on. He doesn't consider that exaggerated put-downs might undermine his own credibility as an objective scientist.

A large body of scientific research attempts to verify spiritual experiences and the paranormal. *The God Delusion* spends little time on impartial research findings and no time objectively weighing the pros and cons on controversies about reincarnation, near-death experiences, and the efficacy of prayer. Beginning in the 1960s, for example, at the psychology department of the University of Virginia, psychiatrist Ian Stevenson headed a long-term study to investigate children who seem to remember their past lives. Typically this happens between the ages of two and seven; it fades quickly after that. From over four decades of research, more than twenty-five hundred case studies have been compiled. The children bring up memories of where they used to live, their friends and family, and the details of their deaths. A number of children in Japan and the United States remember dying in combat in World War II. In one case a little boy got excited seeing a newsreel of fighter planes over the Pacific, and when one went down, he pointed to the television screen and said, "That was me." The family sought out survivors of that particular battle, and they described in detail the pilot whom the little boy thought he was. He got every detail and even a few names right.

Coming from India, I was well aware of such incidents, which are widely known and believed. Children have been tested by taking them to the village they remembered living in, and quite often their recollections of streets, houses, and people are verified. Stevenson pursued these anecdotal stories, and by now the research team that continues his work has amassed hundreds of verified examples from around the world. The most startling examples are probably those in which a child is born with birthmarks that duplicate the wounds, such as where a bullet entered the chest, that correlate to how his previous incarnation died.

An independent study reviewing the data that Stevenson's program gathered came to the conclusion that "in regard to reincarnation he has painstakingly and unemotionally collected a detailed series of cases . . . in which the evidence is difficult to explain on any other grounds." A fascinating subject has been held under scientific scrutiny for anyone to examine. The same is true of every phenomenon that skeptics like Dawkins ridicule rather than investigate. At the very least, experiences that you don't understand deserve to be examined scientifically, especially if you are a scientist. Dawkins considers such research bogus by definition, so all he has to do is cite a single contrary study to avoid even looking at masses of objective research.

Dawkins devotes a few pages to scientists who believe in God. He shrugs off Copernicus, Kepler, Galileo, and Newton immediately because their prestige gives little weight to "an already bad argument." But Darwin, who is Dawkins's household god, should have given him pause. As a young man, Darwin was conventionally religious. In his autobiography he writes, "Whilst on board the *Beagle* I was quite orthodox, and I remember being heartily laughed at by several of the officers (though themselves orthodox) for quoting the Bible as an unanswerable authority on some point of morality." His doubt arose over a conventional question that many other Victorians wrestled with: How could one God countenance the existence of many gods, like Shiva and Vishnu? Did he have separate messages for Hindus and Christians? Darwin found many reasons to doubt that the Gospels were literally true, and after much consideration, he tells us, "I gradually came to disbelieve in Christianity as a divine revelation."

But it isn't on the basis of evolution that Darwin abandoned Biblical religion, which makes for discomfort if you rely on evolution as a mainstay of your atheist position. Darwin didn't consider the issue of a personal God until late in life, at which point he did use natural selection to refute arguments in favor of a benign, loving creator. It is striking how diffident he is when writing about his unbelief. He compares himself to someone who is blind to the color red in a world where everyone else can see red. Thus he understands that "the most usual argument for the existence of an intelligent God is drawn from the deep inward conviction and feelings which are experienced by most persons." As a young man he had the same feelings—in a journal entry from his voyage on the *Beagle*, he recalls being so overawed by the Brazilian jungle that he was convinced that only the existence of God could account for it. But in later life those feelings looked untrustworthy: "I cannot see that such inward convictions and feelings are of any weight as evidence of what really exists."

Without a doubt, he was laying the ground for a modern scientist's reliance on objective evidence alone. But Darwin was far from being a God-basher. After discussing the possibility of immortality and other attributes of God, he says, "I cannot pretend to throw the least light on such abstruse problems. The mystery of the beginning of all things is insoluble to us; and I for one must be content to remain an Agnostic." Dawkins's way of wriggling out of this inconvenient fact is to say that in the nineteenth century the pressure to believe was so great that unbelievers were reluctant to really speak their mind. He quotes Bertrand Russell, a famous atheist among philosophers, to the effect that such pressures inhibited scientists well into the twentieth century: "they conceal the fact in public, because they are afraid of losing their incomes."

Against this conjecture, which seems weak even for Dawkins, he fails to consider that a scientist can believe in God because, as the geneticist Francis Collins says, science is good at commenting on the natural world but not on the supernatural. For Collins as a believing Christian, "both worlds, for me, are quite real and quite important. They are investigated in different ways. They coexist. They illuminate each other."

Does it matter if great scientists believe in God? Copernicus, Newton, and the rest didn't conduct experiments on the existence of a deity. Nor did they rely on direct personal experience (although their biographies reveal some such experiences, as all kinds of people have had). Polling great scientists for their opinions on art wouldn't matter; the two fields are entirely separate.

Since *The Origin of Species* did so much to crush the Bible and Christian belief in general, why did Darwin avoid atheism? A young admirer wrote a letter asking Darwin about his religious beliefs and received a careful reply. It was a study in high-minded fence-sitting. Darwin wrote,

> It is impossible to answer your question briefly; and I am not sure that I could do so, even if I wrote at some length. But I may say that the impossibility of conceiving that this grand and wondrous universe, with our conscious selves, arose through chance, seems to me the chief argument for the existence of God; but whether this is an argument of real value, I have never been able to decide.

This brings us back to chance and probability. In the age of faith, people beheld the intricate patterns in nature and immediately saw the hand of a creator. The rise of science undermined such intuitive perceptions. Every aspect of nature demanded some kind of data. Mathematics trumped "natural religion," as it was called. So let's see which side the probabilities actually favor. Is it more likely that God exists or that he doesn't?

Is God the ultimate 747?

There's a famous answer to that question. In 1982 the British astrophysicist Sir Fred Hoyle gave a radio lecture in which he mentioned in passing that "a colleague of mine worked out that a yeast cell and a 777 airplane have the same number of parts, the same level of complexity." The current scientific explanation for how all the complex parts of a yeast cell came together is randomness. Hoyle tried to calculate how unlikely it was that random chance had assembled a living cell. The odds were very low. But what has survived is a striking analogy that doesn't depend upon whether he got his numbers right (the model of airplane changed along the way):

> The chance that higher life forms might have emerged in this way [i.e., randomly] is comparable to the chance that a tornado sweeping through a junkyard might assemble a Boeing 747 from the materials therein.

The analogy was brilliant because it can be easily understood, and believed, by anyone. A Boeing 747 has around six million parts, and it takes intelligence, design, and planning to fit them all together. Hoyle wasn't a creationist, and he didn't believe in God. His aim was to show that highly complex structures can't be explained by chance.

It's easy to amplify the Boeing 747 junkyard analogy to make it even stronger—a thousand times stronger, in fact: There are six *billion*, not six million, genetic letters strung along human DNA. Their arrangement is precise and delicate. Major impairments like birth defects and genetic disorders can result if the arrangement of even a few genes is imperfect. This implies that an Intelligent Design is present, even though the words *intelligent* and *design* have turned into buzzwords for creationism. Creationism enjoyed a flurry of publicity as fundamentalist Christians dressed up the Biblical creation story in wobbly science. The long-term damage was that it tainted the concept of intelligence in nature.

Dawkins makes hay by aiming chapter after chapter against religious fundamentalists. As he presents it, if you suggest that nature looks designed, you are in the same leaky boat as someone who believes that the Book of Genesis is literally true. Dawkins participates in debates with theologians and emerges unscathed (by his account), since his opponents are befuddled and intellectually outgunned, forced to retreat to musty arguments about God having a special place in nature outside the reach of science. In effect, he says, they put God in a safe zone, making him exempt from scientific reasoning. If he weren't securely tucked away in a safe zone, God couldn't survive the scrutiny we apply to amoebae, electrons, and dinosaur bones.

The Boeing 747 junkyard analogy is too convincing to ignore, however, and *The God Delusion* must face it squarely. As Dawkins writes, "The argument from improbability is the big one." He picks up a religious pamphlet published by the Watchtower Bible and Tract Society—the publishing arm of Jehovah's Witnesses—that defends creationism. The pamphlet cites examples of complex life-forms that indicate the hand of a creator God. One is *Euplectella*, a deep-sea sponge popularly called Venus's Flower Basket. (It is a traditional gift in Asia as a symbol of romantic love, because inside each sponge lives a male and a female shrimp, protected in their nest. When they mate, their offspring swim out into the ocean to find their own nest in another *Euplectella*.) The sponge's skeleton is formed of millions of glass fibers so intricately interwoven that their design has interested the makers of fiber optics; the sponge converts silicic acid, found in seawater, into silica, the chemical basis of glass. The Watchtower pamphlet declares that science cannot explain how such complexity arose: "But one thing we do know. Chance is not the likely designer."

Dawkins intends to surprise the reader by agreeing. Randomness is indeed a bad explanation for the glass skeleton of Venus's Flower Basket, he says. No one would credit that such exquisiteness came about by chance. Dawkins intends to surprise us with this apparent flip-flop, since he relies so heavily on randomness and probability. But he refutes the Boeing 747 junkyard analogy by using it against itself. The problem, he says, is that Fred Hoyle, brilliant as he was, misunderstood evolution completely. The secret of natural selection, the source of its brilliance as a theory, is that it doesn't need random chance. Living things compete selfishly. They take deliberate action. Plants want light and water. Animals want food and a mate. As soon as a liana vine evolves and can twine to the top of a tree in the jungle, it gets the light it craves. A cheetah that evolves loose shoulder joints to enable it to stride longer and faster is going to beat out other big cats chasing after gazelles. Step by step, each living thing earns its right to survive; the steps aren't random at all.

So why, he asks, do our minds keep reaching for God as the designer of the physical world? Because we falsely assume that some things are so beautiful and complex that their design cannot be denied—think of the intricate helix of a chambered nautilus shell or the same spiral helix at the heart of a rose, the double strands of DNA, and the arrangement of seeds in a sunflower. Our eyes tell us that a designer must have devised this beauty and complexity.

Well, yes and no. It's natural to connect a man-made machine like a pocket watch with a maker, says Dawkins. Watches don't assemble themselves. But the same isn't true in nature. Galaxies, planets, DNA, and the human brain did assemble themselves. How? For life to appear on Earth, Darwin shows the way. Intricacy is built up by a sequence of tiny steps. You may stand in awe of a Roman mosaic wall, but if you get close, you'll see that it's made of tiny chips of colored stone. A chip isn't awesome. Darwinism explains that the tiny steps of evolution are not improbable at all; they are the building blocks of everything complex in the natural world. The choice between God and chance is a false one, Dawkins writes. The real choice is between God and natural selection.

If you want to see something really improbable—to the point of laughing it out of existence—look at God. Dawkins calls God "the ultimate Boeing 747 gambit." A God who could create every form of life in one stroke, as the Book of Genesis declares, would have to be more complex than what he created—more complex than DNA, quarks, billions of galaxies, and everything else that emerged over 13.7 billion years since the Big Bang.

It is *extremely* improbable that such a being stands behind the curtain of nature. You can peer at the fossil record and prove the slow, inexorable process of evolution to yourself. Hoyle brought up a red herring when he tossed randomness into the ring. The right answer is that a designer God defies *any* odds. Dawkins cites his atheist colleague Daniel Dennett from Tufts University, who as a philosopher has been given the role of deep thinker in these matters. In a 2005 interview with a German journalist, Dennett addresses "the idea that it takes a big fancy smart thing to make a lesser thing." If you're naïve, this notion seems intuitively right, Dennett says. "You'll never see a spear making a spear maker. You'll never see a horseshoe making a blacksmith. You'll never see a pot making a potter."

Dennett labels this the "trickle-down theory of creation." God is a blacksmith hammering out horseshoes on a cosmic scale. Dennett, whom Dawkins offers up as a "scientifically savvy philosopher," lends credence to the argument of improbability. They both agree that a cosmic blacksmith or watchmaker is too intricate to be likely. Science, when faced with a choice, prefers the simplest explanation that fits. Random chance is too far-fetched, so it doesn't fit. A God who is infinitely complex doesn't fit. What's left is evolution. Case closed.

Perhaps, or perhaps not

In real life, only the tiniest handful of people believe in God because they've waded into the weeds of probability theory. But let's stay with this knotty problem. Do you believe the Boeing 747 analogy? I do. At its crudest, *The God Delusion* turns God into a simplistic caricature. It's absurd to ask whether Jehovah created DNA or not. We must toss out Dawkins's straw man, a personal God who designed the universe. This is just another variant on seeing God as a human being, only much smarter. Many people, as we've discussed, can conceive God only in a human image. When someone runs away from organized religion, this is the God they are rejecting.

Dawkins takes nearly four hundred pages to demolish God without seriously considering that a father in the sky might not be the only way to think about the divine. As soon as you reply, "That's not the God I had in mind," the straw man of God the Father becomes irrelevant. Organized religion has been backed into a corner by its refusal to find a viable alternative to God the Father, but such alternatives do exist. Saint Augustine had already rejected a literal reading of the Bible in the fifth century AD. Modern belief has gone much further away from literalism, but it serves Dawkins not to even take a peek.

One possibility is that God *became* the creation. (Einstein suggested something like this in his famous quote about wanting to know the mind of God, although he didn't explicitly say that God was inside the laws governing time and space.) In other words, God is not a person but the totality of nature. As the source of existence, he is the starting point of your being and mine. God isn't our father; he isn't a watchmaker assembling parts into a watch (an image devised in the eighteenth century to explain how a single intelligent creator put all the moving parts of the cosmos together); he doesn't have feelings and desires. He is being itself. All things exist because he existed first. There is no need for such a God to be intricate.

Setting up a God who must be more complex than the entire universe is merely a ploy. Medieval theologians argued that God had to be more complex than his creation. Dawkins and Dennett should be arguing in the lecture halls of the University of Paris around 1300. In the eighteenth century, the watchmaker analogy became popular because a movement known as deism, which Thomas Jefferson belonged to, wanted to reconcile faith and reason. Deists accepted that God isn't present in the world, and reason told them that miracles can't exist, because they defy the laws of nature. What sort of deity can be worshipped who isn't present and who doesn't perform miracles? A rational god, one who constructed the universe, set it in motion, and then walked away. For Deists, God is like a watchmaker who built his machine, wound it up, and let it run on its own.

The Dawkins twist is to demand that the watchmaker God be more complex than the universe. It's not a demand anyone should accept, for good reason. When you lift your hand to switch on a lamp, you carry out a simple intention. The fact that your brain contains a hundred billion neurons and perhaps a quadrillion synaptic connections is irrelevant. No one needs to examine all those neurons and connections to calculate the probability that they will result in moving your hand. Your intention moves it; the brain's complexity serves the performance of a simple act. Complexity is no obstacle to creating the thoughts, words, and actions that make up the human condition. The brain is too complex for anyone to understand, yet we use it every day.

God could be the simplest thing of all, in fact. He is a unity. Diversity unfolds from this unity, and diversity—the expanding universe, billions of galaxies, human DNA—is bewilderingly complex. But its source doesn't have to be diverse. Picasso was the source of tens of thousands of artworks, but he didn't have to imagine all of them at once in his mind. Like natural selection, God is allowed to produce the natural world step by step, unless you insist, as Dawkins does, that the literal acceptance of Genesis is the only creation story religious people believe in. The alternative I posed, that God became the creation, has a long tradition as well.

The next point that Dawkins makes is quite crucial: complex designs don't need a designer. In a triumphant sentence, *The God Delusion* explains why natural selection is the only successful theory for how life evolved:

> Once the vital ingredient—some kind of genetic molecule—is in place, true Darwinian natural selection can follow, and complex life emerges as the eventual consequence.

Most nonscientists won't spot the sleight of hand here. The Boeing 747 junkyard analogy isn't refuted by what happened *after* life already appeared. What about how DNA got formed in the first place? DNA is a chemical, but in order to explain its structure, you must invoke physics. The sequence of events that led from the Big Bang to DNA is a single chain as far as physics is concerned. The same laws of nature must be at work; there can't be any breaks in the chain, or DNA wouldn't have come about.

It would only have taken a few dropped stitches, billions of years ago, for the whole enterprise to have collapsed—for example, if water didn't emerge from the combination of oxygen and hydrogen. The early cosmos was full of free-floating hydrogen and oxygen, as it is today. DNA cannot exist without water, and the water must have been in abundance for hundreds of millions of years. Since 99.9999 percent of the oxygen and hydrogen in the universe didn't turn into water—add as many decimal places as you like—the fact that water appeared on Earth isn't a matter of tiny probable steps. Quite the opposite—arguments for the uniqueness of life on Earth still hold enormous power, and they don't have to be arguments based on a Biblical God.

The God Delusion offended some scientists as much as it did creationists. They pointed out, in their hostile reactions, that science depends on data, of which Dawkins offers none. He has conducted no experiments and made no calculations in support of his atheistic ideas. The most severe scientific rebuke, however, is that *The God Delusion* doesn't really present a hypothesis that *could* be tested. Its author is wedded to preordained conclusions and has no time for any arguments except the ones that get him where he wants to go.

A distinguished biologist, H. Allen Orr, quotes Dawkins's claim that "we should blame religion itself, not religious *extremism*—as though that were some kind of terrible perversion of real, decent religion." Orr dryly comments, "As you may have noticed, Dawkins when discussing religion is, in effect, a blunt instrument, one that has a hard time distinguishing Unitarians from abortion clinic bombers." Dawkins tries to knock the stuffing out of the Biblical God, but to make sure that he can kick him when he's down, he uses only the most simplistic version of the Biblical God.

If you explore the universe mining it for data and discount everything else, most of what makes life rich and beautiful goes out the window. God isn't a strange supernatural fiction, as Dawkins asserts. He's the source of our inner world, the same place where art, music, imagination, visionary conceptions, love, altruism, philosophy, morals, and human bonding are born. This world has its own truths. We can reach them by experiencing them. Only an alien from another planet would try to prove the existence of love by weighing the probabilities. Only someone who has never seen a platypus would rely on statistics to prove that one couldn't exist. The same goes for Dawkins's approach to God.

THE PATH TO GOD

Stage 2: Faith

Beyond the Zero Point

"I am become Death, the destroyer of worlds." Even many people who have never read the *Bhagavad Gita* recognize this quotation with a shudder. It was spoken by J. Robert Oppenheimer, director of the Manhattan Project, when the first atomic bomb was exploded in the New Mexico desert. He might as well have said, "I am Man, the destroyer of God." The date, July 16, 1945, marks the zero point of faith. A loving, protective God lost all credibility before the unleashed fury of atomic destruction. Very few except the most fervent believers thought that God would—or could—do anything to stop our slide into self-annihilation.

To get beyond the zero point, the nadir of belief, takes focus and effort. Faith must be rebuilt from the ground up. Inertia would simply let it slip away, and then one of the most powerful forces in human existence would be forgotten. What makes the power of faith so remarkable is that it runs contrary to everything we think we know about evolution based on survival. Survival is the ultimate need of every living thing. But human beings answer to multiple needs that are blended into a confusing, shadowy mass. In some cases, we struggle for food, shelter, and family. In other cases, those things are taken care of, and we don't give them a second thought. What makes faith so extraordinary is that sometimes we live for invisible things so intangible that they cannot be put into words. (Can you dissect the difference between "He shows a lot of heart" and "He shows a lot of soul"?)

Yet matters of faith sometimes override every other drive in our lives, even the drive to survive.

In the same year that the atom bomb changed the world, the Allies liberated the concentration camps that had carried out the Final Solution. Scenes of unspeakable suffering were revealed, but so were stories of prisoners who volunteered to die in place of others.

One of the most inspiring examples was a Polish Franciscan friar named Father Maximilian Kolbe, who died at Auschwitz in 1941. The Gestapo had arrested him for harboring Jews in the monastery that he had founded in Niepokalanów; it was a center for publishing Catholic devotional materials in Poland. Photos of him show a resolute man with black-rimmed spectacles and close-cropped hair. He had been a fervent proselyte for the faith and a missionary to Japan. While there, he had built a mountain mission near Nagasaki. Later when the atom bomb destroyed most of the city, the mission was untouched. Kolbe's devotees hinted at divine inspiration because he had chosen to locate it on the side of the mountain that would be shielded from the blast.

Soon after he was transported to Auschwitz in May 1941, some prisoners had successfully escaped, and authorities decided to retaliate. They chose ten inmates to be held in subterranean cells and starved to death. When one of the chosen cried out in anguish, Kolbe stepped forward and volunteered to take his place. He spent the next two weeks praying and leading the other condemned in song and prayer, always facing his tormentors resolutely. The other nine died, but Kolbe still survived. He was summarily executed with an injection of carbolic acid. His body was cremated in the Auschwitz ovens that became synonymous with the worst crimes against humanity.

Father Kolbe's death has always moved me, but it is entangled in the complex fate of modern faith and in the Catholic teaching about martyrs who die for God. His road to sainthood unfolded quickly. By 1950, two miraculous healings were attributed to him. He was beatified in 1971 and canonized in 1982 by Pope John Paul II, a fellow Pole and sufferer at the hands of the Nazis. I've read devotional accounts that Saint Maximilian, as he now is, emitted light when he prayed, and that Jews in Auschwitz stuck small notes into the floorboards of their bunkhouses before they went to their own death, attesting to his supernatural faith.

This sketch of a remarkable believer raises all the paradoxes of faith. Someone who showed the greatest faith was not protected by God but was allowed to die. Instead of his life, it was his death that became the greatest thanks that Kolbe could give to God. Should we have faith in that kind of deity? Children are taught that it is natural to worship God, yet miracle stories make ultimate faith seem supernatural. The enormous divide between the rational and the magical seems unbridgeable here. But the miraculous aspect of saints—as opposed to their saintly behavior—is what appeals most to believers and is most scorned by skeptics.

Kolbe's story demonstrates that the seeds of both unbelief and belief exist in all of us. I have met few people whose faith made God a mighty fortress, as Martin Luther would have it. And I've met few who realized how tender faith can be, as when Tagore says, "Faith is the bird that feels the light and sings when the dawn is still dark." If your heart is touched by those words, you've arrived at one of the deepest spiritual secrets: What is most tender can also be immortal. As long as the heart survives, so will faith.

Losing faith happens one person at a time, and so does regaining faith. I'm approaching faith as the middle stage of renewing God. It isn't the end stage because faith is belief, and belief falls short of knowledge. For some things a middle stage isn't necessary. When you order chocolate mousse in a restaurant, you don't need to test your faith that it will come. But we can all feel the terror of concentration camp victims waiting for God to rescue them. Faith weakens when God doesn't perform to our expectations; it weakens fatally when God seems to pay no attention at all.

By whatever path, when you arrive at the zero point, much the same pattern of disappointment holds true.

The Zero Point of Faith

How did God fail you?

He ignored your prayers.

He allowed you to fall into danger and didn't protect you.

You don't feel divine love.

No mercy was shown to you.

You got sick, and no healing came.

You saw bad people prosper while goodness went unrewarded.

There was abuse and violence in your life, and no one stopped it.

An innocent child died.

Accidents and trauma happened to you without reason.

You suffered mentally through grief, anxiety, or depression, and
God offered no comfort.

Every life has had at least a few of these occurrences and sometimes more. History is a graveyard of unanswered prayers by the millions of people who have needlessly suffered and died. Theology has come up with various excuses: the *Deus otiosus,* or "idle God," whose role ended after the creation; and the *Deus absconditus,* or "hidden God," who is there and not there at the same time. But theology is cold comfort when God does not respond to us under desperate circumstances. Most people believe—understandably so—that God should show his love, mercy, and protection when the going gets tough. We can mostly handle the lesser crises ourselves.

The skeptical alternative

Once you have settled on the zero point, why leave it? If God doesn't exist, it's the most realistic place to be. I don't want to replow the field of atheism, but it does seem rational to take the world as it presents itself. This is the position taken by religious skeptics. God becomes another phenomenon, like the northern lights or cold fusion: *Show me, and I'll believe it.* Skepticism demands visible proof; therefore it's the opposite of faith. A believer doesn't require God to knock at the front door with a government-issued ID.

In our time, the most adamant skepticism has linked itself to science: Before they believe anything, hard-core skeptics want measurable data, experiments with results that can be replicated, and impartial peer review—the whole apparatus associated with the scientific method. If these are lacking, one's belief is likely to be discredited, if not maligned. Skepticism sees itself a realistic, a hardheaded rebuttal of all the superstition, gullibility, and fantasy that holds the world in bondage.

Michael Shermer, the editor of *Skeptic* magazine, quotes with approval a fellow skeptic who deems "the God question—atheist, agnostic, theist, whatever"—to be altogether the wrong question to ask. What makes it wrong? "Gods that live only in people's heads are far more powerful than those that live somewhere 'out there,' for the simple reason that (1) there aren't any of the latter variety around, and (2) the ones in our heads actually affect our lives."

On the list of disappointments that cause people to turn away from God, each item is positive to a skeptic, a wake-up call to face life as it is, not as we wish it to be.

Skeptical Answers for Doubters

Did God ignore your prayer?
Answer: Prayers are never answered at all. What you think inside your head has no effect on outside events.

Did God allow you to fall into danger? Did he fail to protect you?
Answer: The risks you run are your own responsibility. Blaming a higher power signals a failure of self-reliance, if not childish weakness. Nobody who is mature needs a supernatural parent in the sky.

Do you not feel divine love?
Answer: Love is the product of chemical reactions in the brain. It has no existence outside its physical manifestation. The scientific truth is that romantic love may be as much a fantasy as divine love.

Was God's mercy not shown to you?
Answer: Mercy is wish-fulfillment, born of a futile desire to escape the laws of nature. Every cause has its effect. The whole setup is mechanical. There is no free pass from determinism.

Did you get sick and no healing came?
Answer: Disease is a complex process that medical science continues to understand better. One day, as research continues, we will know precisely why certain illnesses befall certain people. At that point, new drugs will solve the whole issue of healing.

Have you seen bad people prosper while goodness went unrewarded?
Answer: What we call good and bad are evolutionary traits

that were developed for survival. Once we understand natural selection more fully, we will know the optimal behavior that holds societies together.

That sampling will give you the gist of how skepticism views the zero point. Every complaint against God has a scientific answer. If current science falls short, there will eventually be a better answer in the future. Over the years I've found that the assumptions of the skeptics are far more pervasive than the arguments of the atheists. The skeptics feel that they occupy high ground because they are necessary to the progress of science. Without a handy skeptic around, we'd all still believe that Zeus throws thunderbolts.

The skeptical point of view earns wide popular acceptance, I think, when it attacks easy targets. *Skeptic* magazine devotes many pages to exposing charlatans, medical fraud, and pseudoscience. It gives almost no space to a serious consideration of speculative thinking about God, the soul, consciousness, and the nature of reality. It draws a fence around conventional, materialistic explanations (which are considered good and true); outside the fence lies the darkness of the deluded mind. Bringing down a medical quack serves a good purpose, no doubt. Exposing con men has marginal value, although it's usually their victims who sound the alarm, not scientific skeptics. But when the skeptical crusade encroaches on genuinely sincere, far-seeing thinkers, it turns noxious. Anyone who champions mind-body medicine, for example, is liable to the same ridicule as quacks. In the 1980s faculty members from medical schools in Boston grew apoplectic whenever I—or any other M.D. interested in alternative treatments—proposed that the mind-body connection was real. The spontaneous remission of cancer was almost totally ignored. (A prominent oncologist told me that cancer was a numbers game; he had no interest in the rare case where a tumor vanished without medical treatment.) Skepticism does general harm by suppressing curiosity, hiding its intolerance behind the excuse that only official sci-entific guidelines are valid when exploring the unknown. One might call this institutionalized curiosity.

God is much harder to get past the skeptics. To them, belief destroys a person's credibility as a rational thinker. And once you use the fatal word *supernatural*, the way is open for contemptuous dismissal. Francis Collins, as I have mentioned, is an eminent geneticist and the director of the National Institutes of Health; he is also a practicing, Bible-believing Christian. Uniquely placed as he is, he will serve as a prime test for faith as it stands next to reason.

Collins recounts the spiritual experience that changed his life in *The Language of God*:

> On a beautiful fall day, as I was hiking in the Cascade Moun-tains, the majesty and beauty of God's creation overwhelmed my resistance. As I rounded a corner and saw a beautiful and unexpected frozen waterfall, hundreds of feet high, I knew the search was over. The next morning, I knelt in the dewy grass as the sun rose and surrendered to Jesus Christ.

There is nothing to be skeptical about in this description of a peak experience, when the everyday world of appearances suddenly changes. For Collins, the meaning of his peak experience was religious, as it would be for almost any seeker. But other minds work in other ways: the famous landscape photographer Ansel Adams had a similar thing happen to him while climbing in the Sierra Nevada, and his interpreta-tion was an artistic epiphany. Both men experienced wonder and awe before nature's grandeur. Collins dedicated his inner life to Christ; Adams dedicated his to photography. A common thread runs through peak experiences: In a sudden expansion of consciousness, the mask of the material world falls away, revealing hidden meaning.

Sam Harris compares Collins (whose scientific credentials exceed

Harris's by an order of magnitude) to a surgeon who has "attempted to operate using only his toes. His failure is predictable, spectacular and vile." Leave aside the hostility. What Harris, and all like-minded skeptics, object to is the mind-set that finds messages in nature, coded communications written in the beauty and design of mountains, sunsets, rainbows, and so on. Scorning the fact that countless people have seen God's hand at work, he comments sarcastically on Collins's experience:

> If this account of field research seems a little thin, don't worry—a recent profile of Collins in *Time* magazine offers supplementary data. Here, we learn that the waterfall was frozen in *three* streams, which put the good doctor in mind of the Trinity.

At this point, Harris remarks, "Thoughts of suicide might occur to any reader who has placed undue trust in the intellectual integrity of his fellow human beings." I don't think so. Most readers would respect the experience as genuine. They might long for a peak experience of their own—I've never heard of anyone who even remotely reacted to one with "thoughts of suicide"—and common sense would tell them that Collins's conversion has nothing to prove to science. As the noted mathematician and physicist Eugene Wigner remarked, "Where in Schrödinger's equation is the joy of being alive?" If I say that I am in love with the most beautiful woman in the world, in what way is a skeptic proving anything when he points out the improbability of finding the one woman out of three billion who is the most beautiful?

Human existence would be fatal without moments of inspiration. In exchange for such moments, when love, beauty, and the possibility of reaching higher reality become vividly true, we endure a great deal of tedium, routine, mundane work, and suffering. But skepticism denigrates inner illumination or tries to explain it away as some kind of brain anomaly. A 2007 article in *Skeptic* magazine reviewed a debate set up between Dawkins and Collins by *Time* magazine. Collins's defense of God rested on a belief that science is powerless to refute: "God cannot be completely contained within nature." As a skeptic views it, this position is a cop-out. It begs the question of whether God even exists and sidesteps the need to offer evidence.

And yet the skeptical position is equally tied to assumptions of its own. Here is how a timeless God looks from the viewpoint of an article in *Skeptic* magazine.

> If there is no time, there is no change. If there is no change, there is no action. If there is no action, there is no creation. If God were to exist outside time, he would be impotent to do anything at all!

This argument assumes that the timeless is a place that we can refer to the way we refer to Pittsburgh or New Delhi. Thinking about anything that lies outside time is so difficult, if not impossible, that it baffles the most advanced physicists in the world. The whole point is that logic breaks down there, and so does the linear world of cause and effect. Collins's belief in a transcendental God permeates every spiritual tradition for a very good reason—the source of nature cannot be found by looking around at nature.

However, the flaws of skepticism don't make faith perfect. In his book Collins asserts that "of all the possible worldviews, atheism is the least rational." This carries weight coming from a renowned scientist, but Collins's exhortation to other fundamentalist Christians jangles against rationality, as most people understand the term: "As believers, you are right to hold fast to the concept of God as creator; you are right to hold fast to the truths of the Bible; you are right to hold fast to the conclusion that science offers no answers to the most pressing questions of human existence." Sir Isaac Newton, a confirmed Christian, might have agreed with every word. Two great scientists could still be religious nuts—but it might not matter: Skepticism has taught everyone to be wary.

It's not a question of twisting science to make it agree with the Bible. The harmony that Collins seeks between science and faith is extremely rational.

> God, who is not limited to space and time, created the universe and established natural laws that govern it. Seeking to populate this otherwise sterile universe with living creatures, God chose the elegant mechanism of evolution to create microbes, plants, and animals of all sorts.

All he asks us to do is keep an open mind. Faith, as it has evolved in the age of science, is about possibilities, not about dogma. If you have an open mind, you will have no trouble with the possibility that something beyond space and time served as the source for the universe. The real issue—and this is where the controversy starts—is whether creation came out of "nothing," that is, a nonphysical source. Is there room in that nothingness for higher organization, the kind of mind that could have perfectly fit the laws of nature together to such a finely tuned degree that the slightest change would have spelled doom for the early universe? After all, with an alteration of less than one billionth in the law of gravity, for example, the nascent universe would have collapsed in on itself after the Big Bang; an alteration in the opposite direction would have caused it to fly apart in uncontrollable winds of proto-gases, never to form atoms and molecules.

The fine-tuning of the universe is indisputable, and we are the direct beneficiaries. Somehow creation emerged in such perfect harmony that human DNA arrived on the scene thirteen billion years later. Because Collins applies religious significance to the problem, he is excluded from the minds of the arch-skeptics. Harris gives him no credit for even holding a rational position. Skeptics never give anyone who thinks differently from them the benefit of the doubt—their minds are closed. But the issue isn't one of fair play. Every new discovery requires faith, including scientific discoveries. The list of things in our lives where we apply faith is impressive.

It Takes Faith . . .

To believe in yourself.

To believe in progress.

To accept that reasoning solves problems.

To trust your emotions.

To reach moments of insight.

To see beyond surface appearances and trust what you see.

To let your body take care of itself.

To feel bonded with another person.

All these things are so basic that we take them for granted, as if having faith in God were altogether different and special, or supernatural and irrational. But the first science experiment in history required all these everyday acts of faith to be securely in place. It's particularly strange that skeptics mock anyone who explores supernatural phenomena, since one item on the list—seeing beyond surface appearances and trusting what you see—is a hallmark of science. Ghost hunters are doing nothing more or less than physicists hunting for quarks.

Believing that the person next to you thinks the same way you do is a huge leap of faith. The brilliant early psychologist William James spoke of "the breach between one mind and another," which cannot be bridged. Two brothers brought up in the same house with the same parenting have almost no chance of thinking the exact same way. One may love hunting and fishing, while the other loves to read Proust. We accept on faith that our minds are connected. But suppose you sneak up behind someone, clap your hands loudly, and get no response. Is the person deaf or simply ignoring you? Is he too absorbed in something else, or is he angry with you? Silence indicates immediately how far apart two minds actually are. Men like to complain that women want them to read their minds (*He*: "Why didn't you tell me that you didn't want to meet my old girlfriend?" *She*: "You should have known."). In fact, we spend our whole lives reading everyone else's mind as best we can.

Then look at what happens when you lose faith in your body. We take nothing on faith more than our hearts, which in a typical lifetime will beat without fail 40 million times a year, or 2.8 billion times in seventy years. The mechanism that sustains a heartbeat is so complex that modern medicine is only now beginning to grasp it. (For the average person, these mechanics, being microscopic, are as invisible and mysterious as God.) But let the heart begin to show signs of distress, as in the chest pains known as angina pectoris, and our faith is shattered. The result, for almost every heart patient, is high anxiety. We suddenly realize that a fist-sized bundle of twitching muscle tissue stands between life and death.

Reducing every aspect of life to facts and hard data is, frankly, preposterous. (We would laugh away anyone who said, "I don't believe you love your children. Show me a brain scan.") The demands of skepticism appeal mostly to the cadre of professional scientists who are bound to strict guidelines when they conduct research. They must examine new results skeptically until viable proof appears. Einstein had to wait for his theory of relativity to be proved by observation, which happened during a solar eclipse in 1919; measurements by the astronomer Sir Arthur Eddington bore out the theory's prediction that light from distant stars would be bent in a curve by the sun's gravitational field. But in that experiment, as in all experiments, the whole point is that science *isn't like real life*. Its constraints are artificial and specialized.

The famous British philosopher Bertrand Russell was an avowed atheist; he made a splash with his 1927 essay, "Why I Am Not a Christian." When Russell was asked how he would defend his nonbelief if he died and wound up in heaven facing his maker, he replied, "Not enough evidence, God, not enough evidence!" Skeptics like to quote that story, but it entirely misses the point. The rules of evidence that apply to material things or events do not apply to God. He can't fail a test he didn't take. Let me explain.

Imagine that a car has run off the road, resulting in a fatal accident in which the driver was killed. The highway patrol show up and find several bystanders. They are asked what happened. The first one says, "See those skid marks? I'm a physicist, and this accident happened because the car's momentum exceeded the force of friction." A second bystander shakes his head. "Look at the position of the wheels. The driver suddenly turned, and the car veered off the road into this ditch. I'm an airline pilot. The accident was caused by veering off course." A third bystander, detecting alcohol fumes from the corpse, announces that he's a doctor, and the accident was caused by drunk driving.

Each bystander has taken a different perspective and offered evidence for it. But notice that there is no scientific way to settle their differences. The answer you get depends upon the question you ask. Perception defines reality. Now imagine that a car rushes up and a distraught woman jumps out, crying, "Fred! You said you would kill yourself, but I never thought you'd go through with it." Her explanation is the right one, because she understands the meaning of the accident. It was caused by the driver's warped emotional state. The lesson here is that descriptions never arrive at meaning. Skeptics, even ones as brilliant as Russell, set up false expectations. No matter what kind of external data you arrive at (skid marks, turned wheels, alcohol in the bloodstream), you can't address the meaning of someone's actions—or the motive for suicide.

Martin Luther King, Jr., gave a reasonable guideline for getting beyond skepticism. "Faith," he said, "is taking the first step even when you don't see the whole staircase." Thinking about Collins's conversion, I came away with some practical principles that are perfectly compatible with rationality yet do not fall under the heavy hand of skepticism:

Faith is personal. It doesn't need to be justified to someone else.

Faith is something you must participate in—you can't judge it from the outside.

Faith is a way of exploring reality, but it doesn't have to pass scientific testing.

Faith looks beyond physical appearances.

Faith is about meaning.

I've gotten only one laugh out of skepticism. I was speaking on spiritual matters to an audience in England. A heckler kept interrupting, and finally he leaped to his feet. "No one should listen to this rubbish!" he shouted. "It's all nonsense."

Taken aback, I asked, "And who are you, sir?"

He straightened himself up. "The head of the British skeptics' society."

"I don't believe you," I said. The audience burst out laughing, and he stomped out of the hall.

A better definition

When God fails you personally, it strikes home. A best seller from the 1980s summarizes loss of faith in its brilliant title, *When Bad Things Happen to Good People.* Whether the bad things befall us at home or in Bosnia or Rwanda, the most basic trust that ties us to God—the promise that good will prevail over evil—frays and then snaps. There is only so much we can take on faith.

I'd suggest that God's failure is not enough to show that he doesn't exist. God can't succeed if he is just a disguise for ourselves—we've already met this deity as God 1.0. Imagine that you've prayed that someone close to you will recover from lung cancer, but she dies anyway. God, like a super doctor whose medicine didn't work, has failed you. He didn't give you what you wanted. You have no way to figure out why. Let's say that the sick person was a chain smoker all her life. Then perhaps God was only being rational. He let the laws of nature, as they operate in the human body, take their normal course.

Or perhaps God chose justice over mercy. It seems fair that someone who ignores every warning about cigarettes and lung cancer shouldn't be miraculously saved. A miracle would be an act of mercy, but what about everyone else who heeded the warnings and then went on to be afflicted with cancer? Should a good shepherd save only the black sheep? We can be sure that a fickle God modeled on human nature can't be real; we constantly judge and blame him when the only thing we're relating to is an extension of ourselves.

The reality of God is hidden behind a fiction of God. Buddha was asked to reassure his followers about the existence of God—who would know the answer better than the Enlightened One? But he took pains not to oblige, because the only viable answer requires a personal journey. It's not easy to get past our imaginary ideas of spirituality, but we have to. It's fascinating to Google the question "Where is heaven located?" One answer, taken from Genesis, is that heaven is the atmospheric envelope surrounding the earth, because God said, "Let the waters abound with an abundance of living creatures, and let birds fly above the earth across the face of the firmament of the heavens" (Genesis 1:20). But there is also Biblical authority for the celestial heavens, where the stars are, and a heaven beyond that, the paradise that is "the abode of God." We are firmly in the realm of God as a person who needs a home somewhere.

The *Catholic Encyclopedia* makes the issue even more complicated.

First, there is the omnipresent heaven, which "is everywhere, as God is everywhere. According to this view the blessed can move about freely in every part of the universe, and still remain with God and see everywhere." This answer gets past the image of a humanized God who lives in one place. But is "place" even necessary? The *Encyclopedia* recognizes a more abstract state, "the happy state of the just in the next life." After theological twists and turns, we arrive at the notion that heaven is a condition of the soul, while some theologians still hold out for the image taught in Sunday school—God, they argue, "should have a special and glorious abode, in which the blessed have their peculiar home and where they usually abide, even though they be free to go about in this world."

These answers all depend on a depressing assumption: that ordinary people will have no direct experience of God. A psychologist was asked why ordinary people who aren't addicted to gambling keep going to casinos, even though they know the odds are stacked against them. "Because every time the slot machine hits," he replied, "they've proved that God loves them." Theology works out its tortuous answers based on the word of great spiritual teachers. The rest of us are left out in the cold. I'd suggest that the whole framework is wrong. In every life God has a chance to succeed when you make a connection with higher reality, the higher self, or higher consciousness—choose any terminology you want. God becomes more secure the stronger your connection becomes.

Then and only then will heaven become real, too. Nor does it have to be the one and only heaven. When people report having a near-death experience, some say that they have seen heaven. The most common description is childlike. Heaven is a green rolling meadow with flowers and frisky baby animals under a clear blue sky. To a skeptic, such an image is too close to pictures seen in children's books to be real. No doubt. But if we place heaven in consciousness—as a "state of the soul"—there is no need for a fixed image or one for adults only. Leave all images aside, and you have the blank slate where any depiction of heaven is viable; the blank slate is consciousness itself.

Laying down conditions

Your faith won't be fully restored until God starts to perform again. His performance must be consistent and reliable. It can't be a game of chance, wish fulfillment, or an imaginary act that proves he loves you. Faith has to get you beyond failed expectations and reopen the possibility that you can rely on God. This places a demand on God, and naturally many people are reluctant to do that. If *demand* is too strong a word, let's rephrase it. When you ask God to perform, you are saying, "I believe you can do it." In that way, faith becomes functional, a working connection.

For centuries anyone who blamed God, even slightly, for a negative event was branded a heretic. Countless innocents suffered torture and death when their only crime was asking questions. The holdover from that horrible era is the guilty thought *What's wrong with me?* that comes to mind when you question the religion of your fathers. When Daniel Dennett says that most religious people are conformists, the point isn't wrong. People display more "belief in belief"—showing allegiance to their religion in order to fit in—than true belief itself.

To be valid, belief must have a basis in reality. The only basis that makes sense to me is to believe in a God who does what he promises to do. Take the elements of the Zero Point of Faith list (on page 62) and reverse them. Faith is justified when

Your prayers are answered.

Goodness prevails over evil.

Innocence isn't destroyed.

You feel God's love.

God protects you.

Providence provides for you.

My position is that all these elements are real aspects of God; therefore we have a right as believers to experience them. We aren't like petulant children stamping our feet until we get what we want; we are asking God to act in his natural capacity. The bond between God and humankind is a living one. If that is true, higher reality isn't far away. There's no set number of miles you have to travel, no fixed length of time on the road, to arrive there. Higher reality is here and now once you are connected to it. It shapes the everyday reality we experience with all its constant demands and challenges. Faith alone will not suffice to bring it into your life. But without faith, you cannot envision what higher reality is. You can't test it or discover where it touches your existence.

I am delighted by poets who transform their inner world into a meeting with the divine. Hafiz (1325–89), a medieval Persian poet in the Sufi tradition, taught the Koran and held court posts. His subject matter was often worldly, reflecting lives of hunting, drinking, and other pleasures. He and other Persian poets came up with wonderful epigrams, such as this one:

> Your soul long ago drowned in the middle of a vast sea
> While you pretend to be thirsty.

Or this one about the purpose of life:

> Time is a factory where everyone slaves away,
> Earning enough love to break their own chains.

Even more strikingly, Hafiz transforms everyday life, conveying the glowing essence that lies behind it. This gives rise to quite startling imagery.

> *To really lose yourself is like holding a gun to your head*
> *And pulling the trigger—it takes guts.*
> *Facing the truth means tying a bag over your head*
> *Until you suffocate—it takes faith.*
> *You have to be brave to follow God's tracks into the unknown*
> *Where so many things can overwhelm and panic you.*

This is the journey of faith rubbed down to raw psychology. Hafiz puts into words the passion and insecurity that fill human existence, and we turn to him because he feels them so urgently. He describes a state where heart and mind join forces to find out the truth of life, down to its very roots. There is no easy projection of a loving father.

> *Trust me and plunge the jeweled dagger into your heart.*
> *This is what it takes to lose yourself.*
> *There is no other path back to God.*

I feel an instinctive truth in such poetry, but how do we turn inspiration into practicality? Hafiz's dagger thrust into the heart evokes the thrill of courage. But the real point is to turn your inner world into a place where you can meet God. Poets feel free to do that. We can, too, once the zero point is loosened up.

Return again to the Zero Point of Faith list (on page 62). For every item on the list, there are several possibilities that can loosen up a stuck notion. Take the first item: *God ignored my prayers.* The skeptical position is that prayers aren't answered at all. Faith doesn't have to promise that your next prayer will be answered. Instead, it offers some new possibilities that open a window to God. Here are some:

At least one of my prayers was answered. I will see if that really happened.

Perhaps the answer to my prayer is not in my best interest right now, and I need to pay attention to other blessings in my life.

Not getting an answer made me realize that my prayer was too selfish and that what I really wanted was much bigger.

Maybe God didn't answer my prayers, but he has answered someone else's. I'll look into it.

Unanswered prayers could be a good thing. Maybe God gave me something better than what I prayed for.

Faith is about new possibilities. Once you realize this, you are freed from extremes of both absolute belief and absolute skepticism. The issue of prayer has occasioned centuries of debate. Atheists claim that those centuries were wasted on a fiction; agnostics shrug and say that the answer is inconclusive. But nothing can be true until it's tested. The possibilities opened by faith are liberating simply by being possible. In every case, a link is forged between the inner and outer worlds. God may be everywhere, as theology says, but he has to get there one step at a time.

How to Have Faith

Escaping the Zero Point

Prayer: Open the possibility that your thoughts have an effect on the world "out there." A prayer is just a special kind of thought. If it makes a connection with the outer world, it may come true.

Accidents: Open the possibility that all events have a meaning. Accidents are events we can't find a reason for. If we expand our vision and a reason is revealed, there are no accidents.

Bad luck: Open the possibility that good and bad are two halves of a single unfolding process. If you can find out the higher purpose of your life, the two halves will make sense. Then luck, good or bad, will be irrelevant.

Suffering: Open the possibility that events are shaped to bring the least suffering. If divine mercy exists, perhaps it allows suffering only so that we can grow and evolve. Then we don't have to wrestle with what caused our suffering. We only have to accept that there is a way out.

Loneliness: Open the possibility that you have never been alone. If there is a comforting presence that exists everywhere, perhaps it lives inside you, not outside. Loneliness is the natural result of feeling empty inside; the cure is inner fullness.

We don't have to stop here—I've only offered a handful of new possibilities. For some people, they won't be satisfactory. To say that suffering is a means to grow and evolve, for example, will make no sense to someone who doesn't believe in the afterlife. Too many horrors remain inexplicable if all we're given is this one life. But I'm not foisting the afterlife on you. When you think about suffering—which for millions of people is *the* deal breaker with God—find your own new possibility. It could even be skeptical: "Suffering is meaningless, but there's a way to live without being destroyed by it." Or "I fear suffering, but there's a possibility that I could get over my fear."

Just keep in mind that your aim is to free up fixed unbelief. You aren't being asked to take a leap of faith. But you can't simply wait for

God to appear. Stuckness is real, and becoming unstuck requires the flow of awareness. Take each item on the Zero Point of Faith list that applies to you, and write down the new possibilities that branch out from it. Be as thorough as possible. For example, there is *I don't feel divine love*. In the Christian West, where every little child knows the melody to "Jesus loves me, this I know," not feeling God's love is a serious reason to give up on him. Yet think of the other possibilities:

You could be more open to being loved by other people, which may open you to divine love.

You could find someone who has felt God's love, either in a book or in real life. Perhaps there are lessons you can learn from their experience.

You might start with the beauty of nature as a connection to a loving God.

You might expand your definition of love. Maybe it's not a warm feeling of affection but good health, well-being, and freedom from care and woe that show divine love.

These aren't proofs of divine love and shouldn't be mistaken for such. Far better to open your mind more and more as the path unfolds, because then you have a real chance for transformation. Hafiz holds out that possibility in another visionary verse:

> *When the mind becomes like a beautiful woman*
> *It bestows all that you want of a lover.*
> *Can you go that deep?*
> *Instead of making love in the body*
> *With other children of God,*
> *Why not seek the true Lover*
> *Who is always in front of you*
> *With open arms?*
> *Then you will be free of this world at last*
> *Like me.*

If you feel touched by these words, you've found the starting point of faith. Faith has been described as a candle in the window, the light that waits for God to see it. Perhaps a better image is one taken from the Indian spiritual tradition. Faith is like a lamp sitting in an open door. It shines out into the world and inside the house at the same time. When the world "out there" is as filled with God as the world "in here," faith has fulfilled its role.

Bad Faith

Bad faith leads us away from God. Many roads do this, and not all call themselves religion. Science can be used as bad faith to undermine belief while offering no good alternative. This isn't the same as labeling science the enemy of faith, because if your aim is to gain true knowledge of God, science may be a great help. You can identify bad faith, by any name, by its results. The God it puts forward doesn't make life better.

Faith, like God, should be testable. A popular evangelist writes, "Faith activates God." Is that true? I can imagine both sides of a football game kneeling to pray for victory (this scene often appears on television), and clearly one team won't activate God, since it is going to lose. In horrific situations where lives are lost, we can't say that those who survived were the ones whose faith activated God. Perhaps it should be the opposite. Perhaps God needs to activate faith. If he doesn't, faith won't have much to show for itself.

Because faith is private, it's tricky and often unfair to say that someone else is guilty of bad faith. What we're concerned with is the path to true knowledge of God. Faith should help open the way. If instead it blocks the way, we can call it bad faith *for our purposes*. This criterion seems to me limited and fair. It would be unfair to intrude where we don't belong, just for the sake of pointing fingers at someone else's strange-seeming cult. All religions began with a small number of the fervent faithful; therefore all could have been branded as cults until they grew so large that they immunized themselves. By our limited definition, bad faith opposes spiritual growth. The leading suspects are three:

Blind faith
Rank prejudice
Pseudoscience

Each of these gives us scope to distinguish between faith as a guide to spiritual growth and faith as an obstacle to such growth. I once had a distinguished patient named Eknath Easwaran who told me more wise things about faith than anyone else I've read or known. A person of refined mind and gentleness, Easwaran—this was his first name—came from Kerala in South India and emigrated to California, where he established a meditation center. (His Wikipedia entry features a picture of him lecturing to a full hall of Berkeley students in the fateful year of 1968. The caption says he was teaching the first accredited course in meditation given at a major university.) He died in 1999 at the age of eighty-eight, having spent his life in devotion to the classic spiritual literature of India.

I was raised by a religious mother and a physician father who placed his faith entirely in science. Over time, although my heart went out to my mother and her way of seeing the world, it was my father's way that I chose to follow. This imposed a division inside me, and during my formative years I simply lived with a divided self—as most people do—paying almost all my attention to practical affairs. Becoming a doctor entails scientific training, and my aptitude for it came easily. I became a living example of something that Eknath Easwaran put very simply, so simply that most of us completely overlook it: "You are whatever your faith is."

He wasn't speaking in religious terms. By faith, he meant the core ideas and beliefs you live by. If you believe that people are good and that life is fair, those ideas don't sit inside you passively like pennies in a piggy bank. They are dynamic; they infuse who you are. You won't need to refer to them the way you look up ideas in a book—in a very real sense, you *are* the sum of your inner conceptions.

The implication, which I wish I had seen years before, is that everyone has faith. Faith lives through them. Human beings walk, talk, eat, and breathe their personal faith. It can be a negative, even destructive faith, as when someone lives for revenge. Defending one's religion by killing infidels is a destructive faith disguised as a positive faith. Easwaran was simplifying a verse from the *Bhagavad Gita* where Lord Krishna imparts to the warrior Arjuna the essence of faith:

> *Everyone's faith comes from the perceptions of the mind.*
> *O Arjuna, the ego-personality is the living embodiment of faith.*
> *Your faith is your identity.*

Suddenly faith is much more far-reaching than simply asking yourself, "Do I believe in God?" If you *are* your faith, almost nothing that happens to you can be left out. It then becomes vitally important to know good faith from bad. Bad faith embodies a set of core beliefs that are countered by good faith. Looking at yourself honestly, you will see a confusing mixture of beliefs that are rooted in bad faith and other beliefs rooted in good faith. Untangling them is an important aspect of making faith work for you as it was meant to.

Blind faith

Every religion has dogmas that become matters of faith, binding the religion into a community. A Muslim believes that the Prophet Muhammad recited the Koran at the command of the archangel Gabriel, who appeared to him one night as he was meditating in a cave above Mecca. Christians believe in the Resurrection and Mormons in the Book of Mormon. The faithful are not to question these exclusive beliefs—they are required to have blind faith.

Enemies of religion tend to conflate blind faith with faith itself, quite unfairly. Innocuous examples of faith get blurred into the extreme wrongs that are justified by blind faith. Christopher Hitchens writes about a defining incident in his boyhood. At school one teacher, a pious widow, was in charge of nature studies and the Bible. She fused the two, Hitchens recalls, when she said one day, "So you see, children, how powerful and generous God is. He has made all the trees and grass to be green, which is exactly the color that is most restful to our eyes. Imagine if instead, the vegetation was all purple, or orange, how awful that would be."

Most of us can recall hearing similar silly things being told to us as children. Adults are guilty of talking down, and it's not hard to imagine that this woman, described as harmless and affectionate, had some fanciful religious ideas (no more fanciful than the notion of heaven as a place where good Christians will one day sit on clouds playing harps). But Hitchens says that he was appalled by what she said—and he had an atheist epiphany.

My little ankle-strap sandals curled with embarrassment for her. At the age of nine I had not even a conception of the argument from design, or of Darwinian evolution as its rival. . . . I simply knew, almost as if I had privileged access to a higher authority, that my teacher had managed to get everything wrong in just two sentences. The eyes were adjusted to nature, and not the other way around.

The last sentence is arguable, but what strikes me about a little boy's epiphany is that something like it occurs in every childhood. The moment comes when you realize that adults make mistakes. This moment is disappointing because life is simpler when parents and teachers are perfect, but it also opens the way for developing your own self. In short order, Hitchens began to question other "oddities," as he calls them.

If God created all things, for example, why should he be praised for doing what came naturally? "This seemed servile, apart from anything else." If Jesus could heal the blind as he chose, why didn't he cure blindness itself? As for Jesus hurling out devils that entered a herd of pigs, "that seemed sinister: more like black magic." These questions are precocious, but Hitchens also had more commonplace doubts. "With all this continual prayer, why no result? Why did I have to keep saying, in public, that I was a miserable sinner? Why was the subject of sex considered so toxic?" Certainly these troubling questions have led many people to a loss of faith, although that doesn't mean they cannot be answered. Hitchens made the leap into total shutdown in matters of religion thanks to another school incident:

> The headmaster, who . . . was a bit of a sadist and a closeted homosexual . . . was giving a no-nonsense talk to some of us one evening. "You may not see the point of all this faith now," he said. "But you will one day, when you start to lose loved ones."

This may seem like another example of harmless piety and a correct insight into human nature. It could have come from a kindly teacher who wasn't a sadist or closeted (presumably those tags were gratuitously thrown in to impugn the speaker's character). Millions of people have sought solace from grief through their faith. But Hitchens recalls that he felt a stab of indignation and disbelief. The headmaster was basically saying that "religion might not be true, but never mind that, since it can be relied upon for comfort. How contemptible."

It's good to go back and reexamine the ideas that occur to us as children—especially if they are delivered, as Hitchens's was, as if from a higher authority. But children are impressionable, and formative experiences stick. In this case, even though he was a professional writer and thinker, Hitchens never abandoned his first bout of indignation. He didn't consider that religion might be simultaneously comforting and true—the two are mutually exclusive in his view. Blind disbelief has this in common with blind faith: Both turn to zealotry through black and white thinking. (It's worth noting that contempt and indignation became signature tones in Hitchens's writing career.)

Blind faith and blind unbelief have other things in common. They both refuse to be tested. They condemn the other side. They depend on strong emotional attachments. The main difference is that unbelief disguises its blindness behind a veil of reason. Thus Hitchens says that prayer brings "no result." This discounts the countless people who declare that their prayers have been answered. A reasonable person would take this into account as evidence. Yet the fact remains that most articles of blind faith are not subject to testing for truth or falsity. The Holy Trinity, the Immaculate Conception, Muhammad's ride to Jerusalem on a flying horse and subsequent ascension to heaven—the call of atheists to reject all religion on the basis of its unproven dogmas misses the point. Dogma is like an entry pass or club membership. Most people are born into a religion and therefore automatically have a pass.

Only later do they have a chance to examine the dogmatic side of their faith. Then three salient questions arise: *What do I have to do? How much does it matter? Will I be affected?* Take the most basic of Christian dogmas: that Jesus died and was resurrected from the tomb. This isn't a belief that can be tested; you accept it blindly if you want to be a practicing Christian in most (but not all) denominations. To an outsider, accepting the Resurrection may seem irrational. But if you subject it to the three questions listed above, this article of blind faith exists for more reasons than its believability to a rational person.

What do I have to do? For the vast majority of Christians, the answer is nothing. Belief in the Resurrection is passive except when Mass is taken, and that is voluntary.

How much does it matter? This is a more ambiguous question, since the Resurrection is connected to the forgiveness of sins, a subject that presses close to home for Christians. Also, as a matter of conscience, believing in the Resurrection is a pretty fundamental test—it's hard to consider yourself a Christian if you wholeheartedly disbelieve that Jesus rose from the dead. Yet even here the either/or thinking of militant atheists doesn't apply. Modern theology makes room for faith that lives side by side with doubt, and many denominations long ago turned away from mystical events like the Resurrection in favor of doing good works and living a moral life.

Will I be affected? Just because it is mystical, the Resurrection affects Christians after they die, primarily, and go to heaven. Only then will they discover if Christ redeemed them from their sins. Even then, dogma isn't uniform. Some denominations don't teach about sin and redemption and they place little emphasis on Judgment Day. You can be a practicing Christian, in short, without being affected by the Resurrection.

A popular evangelical saying holds that "Faith activates God." If that's what it takes for God to be present, the stakes are higher than the minimal faith that many Christians feel. Without faith, God will remain inert; the Almighty, who has asked you to take things on faith that in your heart of hearts you don't believe, will ignore you. I reject this quid pro quo setup. A God that accepts one person and rejects another cannot be divine, because, as we've seen, he would be just imitating human nature. In this book, the criterion of faith is different from blind acceptance. Faith is a stage on the way to true knowledge of God. By that standard, blind faith is questionable but not fatal—far from it. As a mystical act, blind faith can open up subtle aspects of the mind. It can lead to an expanded view of reality and allow a person to see himself or herself as multidimensional, existing on other planes beyond the physical.

Blind faith has served such purposes for many centuries. No doubt the rise of science has lessened the power of dogma. On the whole, that's to the good. Testable faith will be much more valuable than untestable. We can't contest the damage done by superstition and ignorance in the history of religion. On the whole, blind faith deserves to be considered bad faith. But equating religion with spirituality isn't valid. You can question blind faith and reject it without doing harm to your spiritual journey. Indeed, you would probably help yourself along the way.

Rank prejudice

When religion creates divisions of intolerance and hatred, it is obviously guilty of bad faith. Southern churches—piously justifying slavery before the Civil War, then turning a blind eye to racial injustice for a century afterward—used God as a mask for rank prejudice.

Some religious teachings actually consider it *necessary* for faith to be prejudiced. Several years ago I was doing research for a book on Jesus and sought out the writings of a recent pope (whose name doesn't need to be singled out). I casually turned to the index reference under "Buddha" and read the following opinion: *Although some people see parallels between the lives of the Buddha and of Jesus, this is a false belief. Buddhism is a form of paganism, believed in by those who have not yet accepted that Jesus Christ is the savior of the world.* Another pope, when he was a cardinal, wrote the encyclical condemnation of Eastern meditation that became church doctrine, on the grounds that meditation took Catholics away from praying to the Virgin Mary as intercessor with God. This reactionary posture saddened me. It is all too prevalent in dogmatic faiths. Whatever the Bible or Koran condemns—be it infidels, gay people, eating prohibited foods, or treating women as equals—cannot be challenged. Orthodoxy, when it turns into rank prejudice, is proud to ignore the changing times. Attitudes never evolve beyond the date of ancient scriptures.

Religious intolerance has to be dealt with in every society and kept from harming other people. Most believers won't feel that the issue comes near to their lives. The courts will be there to order blood transfusions for seriously ill children over the religious objection of their parents or to uphold women's rights. Religion, in all its variety, will step into the marketplace of ideas as one voice among many for cutting-edge change like gay marriage. Yet for all that, these issues do come near us as trials of conscience. I must state my own bias here. Any form of us-versus-them thinking strikes me as bad faith. Religions draw into tight camps where their God is the only true God, for racial, tribal, political, and theological reasons. I find none of them justified.

We all know true believers who reject and even denigrate other faiths. Radical Islam has done great harm to general tolerance for all faiths, just as anti-Semitism has for many centuries. My aim isn't to impose my bias on anyone else. People remain prejudiced for irrational reasons; the best that can be said is that religion is only one ingredient in the mix. Family upbringing often fosters more intolerance, I would imagine, than Sunday school. Rank prejudice belongs to the underbelly of religious culture far more than to its official teachings. The wise course is to let prejudice be what it has always been, a test of conscience. Each person must decide his own limits; each must take a stand according to her own circumstances. As a general topic, rank prejudice is bad faith in its most egregious from. The fact is known to everyone, so not much discussion is needed.

On the other hand, there is much to say about pseudoscience, a form of bad faith that occupies believers and unbelievers alike. Dawkins and company label someone else's serious inquiry quackery if its thinking contradicts their narrow brand of science. In turn, militant atheism misuses the scientific method for its own agenda. The term *pseudoscience* changes depending on what angle you look at it from.

Science takes faith, too

You can make the argument that science should be atheistic in the most literal sense: It should leave God out entirely. God can't be squeezed into a scientific model. It isn't possible to subject him to experimental testing, and therefore Dawkins's claim that God doesn't meet the rigors of science is a blind alley. By the same token, the universe can be measured and explored without bringing in matters of faith.

But of course the simmering feud between science and faith runs deeper than the rise of militant atheists or their avowed opponents, the creationists. Their sideshow has little resonance in the laboratory. Bestseller lists don't necessarily reflect reality. By any realistic standard, the number of people who crusade for either side is small. It distresses scientists far more that so many Americans—more than half, according to one poll—believe that creation could not have taken place without at least some participation by God. (If it helps at all, I imagine that this belief is passive, much like believing in UFOs and the yeti.)

The deeper reason for science facing off against religion in our day is that reality has become too difficult to explain using even the most complex mechanistic models. The hard and fast line that used to divide science and mysticism has become hopelessly blurred. Could the universe be as alive as we are? Might it be capable of thinking? A hint comes in a quote from the late British physicist David Bohm: "In some sense man is a microcosm of the universe; therefore what man is, is a clue to the universe." Humans have always looked to nature as a mirror of ourselves. If we really are a microcosm, then the macrocosm—the universe at large—must be seen in terms of what makes us human.

Suddenly one sees a rash of books by credentialed physicists arguing in favor of a conscious universe, a living universe and even a universe shaped by human perception. This poses a radical challenge to scientific materialism. It might seem that Einstein was in a poetic mood when he declared that he wanted to know the mind of God. It's a serious speculation, however, when Freeman Dyson writes, "Life may have succeeded against all odds in molding a universe to its purposes." In other words, since the only universe we can know anything about comes to us through our minds, it may be that our minds shape reality. A red filter makes everything look red, and if other colors exist, they can't be known as long as you are looking through a red filter.

Looking through the human mind is more complex than holding up a piece of colored glass, but the same limitation holds. Our minds look at a baseball player hitting a home run and, being linear, perceive that the bat has to hit the ball before it can sail over the fence. Simple cause and effect tells the tale. But we know from quantum physics that at a deeper level time goes backward, and that the cause can be assigned after the effect takes place. So it is possible that cause and effect wouldn't exist without a mind geared to see things that way. If you are wedded to an outdated kind of materialism, such a statement sounds absurd. The habit of looking into the mirror of nature stopped making sense when everything "out there" consisted of bits and pieces of data—all breadcrumbs and no loaf.

We need to be clear about a very basic point: The visible universe isn't the same as reality. When solid objects are reduced to atoms and then to subatomic particles, they are no longer solid. They are clouds of potentiality. As physics defines it, potentiality is neither matter nor energy but completely intangible, no matter how solid a mountain may be or how powerful a lightning bolt. Particles in such a state aren't even particles anymore. They do not have a specific location in space; instead, every particle emerges from quantum waves that can extend infinitely in all directions. Even if Dawkins could rescue the notion that what you see is the benchmark for what is real, the most recent theories of the cosmos propose that only 4 percent of the universe is made up of matter and energy that can be measured—the remaining 96 percent consists of so-called dark matter and energy, which are little understood. They cannot be seen, only inferred.

Physicist Joel Primack, who specializes in how the universe is constructed, offers the image of an ice cream cake, a "cosmic dessert" with a makeup that will astonish anyone. Most of the cake, 70 percent, is dark energy, sandwiched with dark matter (25 percent) like chocolate cake and ice cream. Primack chooses chocolate because it is dark, while in reality dark matter and energy have never been observed. This leaves only 5 percent of the cosmos that could be visible. Most of that (4.5 percent of the total) is taken up by floating atoms of hydrogen and helium, along with various mixed atoms in deep space—call this the icing. All other visible matter, which includes stars and galaxies by the billions and billions, are like a sprinkling of cinnamon on top of the cake. The universe upon which materialists base reality, in other words, counts as 0.01 percent of the cosmic dessert.

All the evidence points in one direction: We need a new paradigm for explaining the cosmos. We need to accept first and foremost that the last things to be trusted are the five senses. More than that, even cherished theories like relativity have become drastically unstable. Dark energy is enlarging the space between galaxies faster than the speed of light. So *something* beyond space and time serves as the major force for creation and destruction in the cosmos, and whatever it is, it will be as invisible as mind, God, the soul, and higher consciousness.

For decades, the outspoken British biologist Rupert Sheldrake has worked with courageous vision to bring about a new paradigm; in the process he's made himself a lightning rod for materialists who cannot abide the notion that invisible things might be real. Sheldrake wrote a telling article on why bad science is like bad faith: "Bad religion is arrogant, self-righteous, dogmatic and intolerant. And so is bad science. But unlike religious fundamentalists, scientific fundamentalists do not realize that their opinions are based on faith. They think they know the truth. They believe that science has already solved the fundamental questions. The details still need working out, but in principle the answers are known." This is exactly the position taken by Dawkins; he and his cohorts pursue a faith based on scientism, the belief that the scientific method will one day solve all problems.

As a brand of faith, scientism seems more appealing than, say, creationism, which denies the evolution of the universe and life on Earth. But as Sheldrake points out, scientism has the harmful effect of suppressing thinking and research in any direction that doesn't conform to conventional guidelines. "Science at its best is an open-minded method of inquiry, not a belief system. But the 'scientific worldview,' based on the materialist philosophy, is enormously prestigious because science has been so successful."

If science is a belief system, as faith-based as religion, then it betrays its own principles. It becomes pseudoscience. But the average person—including the average working scientist—has no idea, really, of how much faith science actually takes. Sheldrake writes, "These materialist beliefs are often taken for granted by scientists, not because they have thought about them critically, but because they haven't. To deviate from them is heresy, and heresy harms careers." Sheldrake has written brilliantly on the beliefs that all of us tend to take for granted because of the prestige of science. Let me condense these beliefs into a few sentences:

Science as a Belief System

What you must take on faith

The belief that the universe is a machine whose working parts can be explained and diagrammed. Once that is accomplished, we will have a Theory of Everything.

The human body is also a machine, and science will one day understand every aspect down to the molecular level. Once that is accomplished, disease will be eradicated. In addition, all mental disorders will be cured with drugs.

> Nature is mindless, the product of random activity at
> the physical level. Science will one day convince us to stop
> believing that life has any innate purpose other than survival.

> The evolutionary struggle for food and mating rights
> explains how human behavior arose. Modern behavior is a
> direct result of Darwinian evolution. Our genes determined
> our destiny.

> The mind can be reduced to physical processes in the
> brain. Since these processes follow strict laws of chemistry
> and physics, our lives are deterministic. Free will plays no part
> or perhaps a very minor one.

In this belief system anything tangible has priority over anything intangible. Dawkins belongs to the camp that traces every aspect of human psychology to natural selection. This, too, is pure faith. There are no fossils of behavior, which is fortunate for Dawkins, because none of his theories can be tested. If he claims that God arose as a survival mechanism, there is nothing either to prove or disprove the notion. The way is open for the most fanciful suppositions. Let's theorize that Paleolithic women started to wear necklaces because that attracted more powerful males, who then brought these women an extra mastodon steak as opposed to women who wore only earrings. Dawkins's brand of evolutionary psychology traces behavior back to nothing more than made-up stories like this one.

Unless you have faith that Darwin must apply to everything we think and do, it is obvious that his theory doesn't. Natural selection means that a particular trait makes you better at getting food or fighting for a mate. In what way does cave painting achieve either goal, or the love of a mother for her baby, or the pleasure we get from music? The general public has no idea how rigidly the belief in evolutionary psychology is clung to. Religionists are accused, rightly, of arguing backward from God as a given which has to be true. Because God must exist, a fundamentalist Christian can see God's hand in plane crashes, hurricanes, or the divorce of a Hollywood star. Anything at all can be made to fit their sin-and-damnation scheme.

Science is supposed to be the exact opposite of arguing from faith, yet for Dawkins, the most improbable aspects of human behavior become survival mechanisms. I smile reading Oscar Wilde's quip, "Always forgive your enemies. Nothing annoys them so much." Nobody can possibly prove that humor developed in our ancestors through a random genetic mutation. And how did such a mutation help them to survive? Maybe they got better at picking up girls at Stone Age singles bars. When he scoffs at faith for not being based on facts, Dawkins could aim the same accusation at his own field.

Sheldrake dissects the unproven assumptions of materialism at length in his book *Science Set Free,* which goes a long way to dismantling a worldview that is seriously fraying around the edges. He is realistic about the shortcomings of human nature: "In both religion and science, some people are dishonest, exploitative, incompetent and exhibit other human failings." But his conclusion is that science is being held back by "centuries-old assumptions that have hardened into dogmas."

Does that really affect how we think about God? Yes, quite directly. A universe that is meaningless can't be divine. Random activity undermines all sense of purpose. A mind that arose out of electrochemical activity can't know revelation or epiphany. The choice, for once, does come down to either/or. To me, it is self-evident that spiritual experiences exist, that we act out of free will, and that our lives have meaning. One might claim, with deep conviction, that "natural religion" grew out of human experience, age upon age.

Which means that science has a perfect right to be a belief system, too. The only demand one can make is that scientists own up to their articles of faith. Science doesn't describe reality, because no school of philosophy has ever proved that the physical universe is real. (Even Stephen Hawking, no believer in God, has attested to this.) We assume that physical things are real, on the evidence of the information that enters through the five senses. But that is the same as saying that we accept reality subjectively. Without sight, sound, touch, taste, and smell, there is no reality to experience.

The surprising result is that God is on a level playing field with stars, galaxies, mountains, trees, and the sky. None of them can be objectively validated. "This rock feels hard" is no truer than "I feel God's love." But it's no less true, either, since feeling is one sure way to navigate through the world. If feeling that fire is hot and should not be touched is reliable, then feeling God's love has the same claim to be reliable. What makes it seem unreliable is only a shift in worldviews. We are all embedded in the worldview of materialism; therefore the assumption that spiritual experiences must be unreal has become an article of faith.

The enormous question "What is reality?" will figure prominently in later pages, when we get to the topic of true knowledge about God. All of us, whether scientist or believer, are led by reality. Wherever it takes us, we must follow. The discovery of fossils changed faith forever, as it led the mind into a new model of reality. At this moment, the same thing is happening thanks to discoveries in all kinds of fields, including biology, physics, neuroscience, and genetics. A new model of reality is being shaped, and in turn it is shaping us.

But change hasn't overturned an ancient sentence from the Bible: "For as he thinks in his heart, so is he" (Proverbs 23:7). In other words, we are what our thoughts have made of us. My friend Eknath Easwaran was echoing that sentence in his view of faith as the invisible core inside everyone. Even older than the Hebrew Bible is the Indian concept of *shraddha,* which is usually translated as "faith" but which includes everything we value, strive for, and envision. Saint John of the Cross wrote, "In the evening of life, we will be judged on love alone." In his world of Catholic devotion, the universe was created as a gift of God's love, and our response to the gift indicates our worthiness to receive it. There is no need, however, to translate this truth in religious terms. *Shraddha* tells us that we live by what we love. To love God isn't different from loving science, if that is what shapes your life at its very core.

In bad faith, we insist that our beliefs should define reality for everyone. In good faith, we make the most of what we love and desire no less for everyone. In the *Bhagavad Gita,* Lord Krishna shows a sublime confidence in the power of reality to lead us where we need to go: "As people approach me, I take them into my love. All ways follow a path to me" (*Gita* 4:11). I call this the power of reality rather than the power of God, since an omnipresent deity must be inside every grain of reality, expressing itself through every experience. Sheer mysticism? Only if you choose not to test it. The highest use of free will is to see if it actually leads to God. Krishna limits his powers by saying that if a person chooses no path, there is nothing God can do. The secret of human nature, fortunately, is that all of us follow the path of what we love the most.

For the moment, faith is a way station. Eknath Easwaran looked deep enough into his own life to believe one more thing: When a person is devoted with complete faith, the object of devotion is achieved. It doesn't matter that he found this idea in the *Gita.* What matters is that his life was long enough—and full enough—to prove that it was true.

The Wisdom Agenda

Faith makes life better. That's the proposition before us. On the face of it, the proposition seems shaky. Faith quite often doesn't bring the rewards that have been promised over and over. Empty-handed faith may lead to disillusionment or a broken heart. A touching example comes to mind. The world was shocked when the letters of Mother Teresa, long withheld by the Church, came to light in 2007. The diminutive Albanian nun had died ten years before. Her work with the poor in Calcutta made her a model of Christian charity far beyond the boundaries of Catholicism. Psychological experiments done at Harvard used films of Mother Teresa holding sick, orphaned babies in her arms and showed them to groups of subjects. Merely viewing these images caused beneficial physiological changes, decreasing blood pressure and offsetting various measures of stress.

Suddenly her letters revealed that this saintly figure was wracked with doubts, which had tormented her at the beginning, middle, and end of her career. The former Agnes Bojaxhiu received the Nobel Peace Prize in 1979, but that same year she wrote a letter to a priest with a desolate message in it.

Jesus has a very special love for you. As for me, the silence and the emptiness is so great that I look and do not see, listen and do not hear.

Those who campaign to see Mother Teresa canonized claim that her doubts make her an even more heroic exemplar of faith. (So strenuous was her spiritual struggle that she used a cilice, the proverbial hair shirt or rough undergarment, the discomfort of which reminds the wearer of Christ's suffering.) But if you take the letters literally, at face value, Mother Teresa had a knotty predicament. She tried to live according to a Christian ideal, only to be baffled when God didn't listen or answer her. God never showed his presence to a great devotee, and therefore she had to confront deep disappointment and (as some atheists gleefully point out) unresolved skepticism about the truth of religion.

When belief is great, doubt is never far away. Too much is at stake. Even though she was an outsize personality and a model of immense compassion, the "saint of the gutters" wasn't all that different from ordinary believers who feel that God has abandoned them. Mother Teresa's story reinforces my core conviction: Faith has to make your life better in order to be valid. The legacy of religion can be viewed from afar, in terms of great historical epochs, but ultimately it comes down to how people of faith have fared, one person at a time. If living a saintly life at the service of others leaves you in a state bereft of God, your well-being hasn't improved. If holding fast to religion creates the basis for intolerance—much less torture and war—then an evil has been hatched in the world. The proposition that faith brings a better life fails.

What saves faith from this grim analysis is a counterforce: wisdom. Wisdom supports faith, because both are about invisible things. Both must be tested one person at a time to see if they are valid. When you decide to live in good faith, what happens next? Life happens, between breakfast and dinner. What you think, say, and do has to be shaped into something valuable. The whole question of value is where wisdom applies. Every fork in the road, however small, requires a choice. The world's wisdom traditions provide a guide, based on thousands of years of human experience, as to which choices enhance life the most. Let me give you a general sense of where wisdom points.

Wise Choices

The decisions that shape a conscious life

When you are afraid and anxious, don't trust the voice of fear.

When you are in a chaotic situation, find a way to bring order and calm.

When faced with an angry conflict, make no decision until the anger has subsided. When you meet resistance to your cherished ideas, consider the viewpoint of those who resist you.

When you are tempted to condemn someone else, see if what you hate in them is hidden away in yourself.

When you are in trouble, decide if the situation is one you should put up with, try to fix, or walk away from. Having decided, act accordingly.

When you know the truth, speak up for it.

These are just some examples of wisdom in action; they apply to everyday situations rather than great spiritual issues. There is a story in the Vedic tradition about a young man who went in search of the secret of abundance. For many months he traveled through the countryside until one day, deep in a forest, he met a spiritual master and asked how to make his dreams come true.

"What do you really want?" the master asked.

"I want to have untold wealth, but not for selfish reasons," the young man replied earnestly. "I want to use it to help the whole world. Can you please tell me the secret to creating such abundance?"

The master nodded yes. "In the heart of every human being there are two goddesses. Lakshmi, the goddess of wealth, is generous and beautiful. If you worship her, she may bestow you with treasures and riches, but she is capricious and may also withdraw her favors without warning. The other goddess is Saraswati, the goddess of wisdom. If you venerate Saraswati and dedicate yourself to wisdom, Lakshmi will become jealous and pay more attention to you. The more you seek wisdom, the more fervently Lakshmi will chase you, showering you with wealth and abundance."

This advice goes beyond common pieces of wisdom that one might hear today, such as "Do what you love, and the money will come" or even "Follow your bliss." The lessons of wisdom aren't always blissful, and what you love can change. At a deep level, devoting yourself to Saraswati or wisdom is about connecting to who you really are, discovering and then using what is unique about you. In yourself is the path to fulfillment. Take an external path instead, and all the rewards of money, status, and possessions can end up being worthless, because you haven't really tapped into what would truly fulfill you. But telling someone that money doesn't buy happiness is futile—what it does buy feels good enough. The real problem is mental programming. If you have no other imprinting except materialism, the road less traveled doesn't even exist. They tore it up to build a superhighway to the shopping mall.

As with God, wisdom is valid only if it's practical from day to day. But wisdom also has long-range goals, and these too are the result of decisions. Every spiritual tradition values the goal of peace over conflict, love over fear, understanding over judgment, good over evil. The reason we fail to achieve these long-range goals isn't a lack of vision. Libraries are stuffed with volumes of wise teachings. Rather, the failure is due to the short-range decisions we make between breakfast and dinner. They shape our behavior, attitudes, beliefs, and even our brains.

The brain is predisposed, in a remarkable way, toward making decisions that favor goodness, and from an impossibly young age. Solid evidence has been gathered by the Infant Cognition Center at Yale University, where babies are tested to see if they have an innate moral sense. In one experiment a baby is shown a scene enacted by three dolls. One doll is trying to open a box, but the lid is too heavy for him to handle alone. The doll on the right helps him, and together they get the box open. The doll on the left slams the lid down instead, refusing to help.

After the baby has seen this little drama, he or she is offered a choice. Would it like to play with the "good" doll or the "bad" doll? Over 80 percent of the time, babies will reach for the good doll. This is for babies as young as three months old. Similarly, if an infant who has barely gotten beyond the crawling stage sees his mother drop something on the floor, he will voluntarily pick it up and offer it to her. We can speculate on where this predisposition for good behavior comes from, but it constitutes the seed of wisdom. Not that the situation is so simple that babies are always good. The Yale baby lab also conducts an experiment in which a "bad" doll is punished, and babies show a tendency to favor the punishment rather than to forgive the bad doll. From infancy we have a predisposition not to forgive. This may be the seed of us-versus-them thinking, which some researchers believe is also innate.

The seed of goodness, if it is going to grow, takes years of teaching and experience. Nurturing the good takes place invisibly, and you must have faith to keep moving forward. Viewing our times from the outside—like the proverbial Martian landing in his spaceship to examine the human species—we see that highly visible things like war, crime, and violence trump wisdom. The great new savior is technology, and if 80 percent of college graduates in China are engineers, that shows what a forward-looking society China must be. Ask anyone what they think the solution to global warming, overpopulation, or the worldwide AIDS pandemic will be (pick your own crippling dilemma), and almost certainly they will say that their hopes are pinned on a future scientific breakthrough. The number of people who expect us to be saved by wisdom will be very tiny indeed.

That is shortsighted, however. Despite the treachery of history, wisdom has thrived in the struggle against human folly. The nature of wisdom is that it gathers from the inside, creating a shift in the direction of higher consciousness. We are visionary creatures. Our instinct is to move toward the light. What does the poet William Blake mean when he says, "And throughout all eternity, I forgive you and you forgive me"? The statement is nonsense if you focus on the war and strife that litter bloody history. But if you are convinced that goodness prevails, it's wisdom. When the Frank family were hiding out from the Nazis who occupied Amsterdam and hunted down their Jewish population, Anne Frank wrote in her diary, "Despite everything, I believe that people are really good at heart." Is that credible once we know that the Gestapo eventually found the Franks and sent them to die in Auschwitz—and on the very last train that departed from Holland? In the concentration camps, prisoners died from the horrendous medical experiments performed by sadists like Josef Mengele, Auschwitz's "angel of death," yet with their last breath rare individuals blessed their tormentors. Such extraordinary behavior prevails over pain and suffering, even in the face of certain death.

Wisdom, instead of calculating good versus evil, considers the deeper value of life. We are applying wisdom, for example, when we raise children. A baby has an absolute status; in a good family it is an object of unquestioned love. As the baby grows, the parents teach right from wrong. But they never say to their child, "The fact that you exist is wrong" or "You have brought more wrong into the world than good." This isn't blind love; it's just how love is supposed to be. Wisdom tells us so.

Wisdom is the ability to look beyond the surface of things. No ability is more valuable. On the surface, a two-year-old throwing a tantrum is exasperating. As she screams bloody murder in the supermarket, the child's mother looks embarrassed. People are staring with frowns on their faces. The mother sees in their eyes that they think she's a bad mother or can't control her child. This is a moment for wisdom, which says that young children must be tolerated, guided, and loved for who they are, not judged for how they behave. Beyond the appearance of the situation, the mother understands that "the terrible twos" are just a phase.

Some mothers cannot base their reactions on wisdom. They grow angry at the child. They blame him for causing a scene. They resort to scolding or physical punishment. Their first thoughts are about their own embarrassment and how bad they look in other people's eyes. In other words, such mothers are trapped in the superficial appearance of the situation. They are unable to see beyond it.

We consult wisdom in all kinds of situations where gathering evidence isn't applicable. Wisdom sees what can't be seen with the naked eye. God is a lofty example, but there are many situations that only wisdom can resolve. For most people, the first person in the Old Testament who comes to mind as wise is King Solomon. In the most famous tale about him, two prostitutes appear before him in a bitter dispute. As one tells the story, she gave birth to a son in the house where both women lived. Three days later the other gave birth, too, but in the night she rolled over and crushed her baby to death. Getting out of bed, she exchanged her dead baby for the living one. No one else was in the house except the two of them. The second prostitute says that this is all a lie. So who was the real mother of the living son?

No doubt it was expected, since the king stood in for God, that Solomon would divine who was telling the truth. Instead, he set up a test.

> Then the king said, "Bring me a sword." So they brought a sword for the king. He then gave an order: "Cut the living child in two and give half to one and half to the other."
>
> The woman whose son was alive was deeply moved out of love for him and said to the king, "Please, my lord, give her the baby! Don't kill him!"

But the other said, "Neither I nor you shall have him. Cut him in two!"

Then the king gave his ruling: "Give the living baby to the first woman. Do not kill him; she is his mother." (1 Kings 3:24–27)

The Bible doesn't explain what made the judgment of Solomon so wise, only that it was greeted with astonishment. "When all Israel heard the verdict the king had given, they held the king in awe, because they saw that he had wisdom from God to administer justice." Today we might say that Solomon understood human nature. He knew that the real mother would rather give up her baby than see it die. Yet there is something else. Wisdom is a surprise; it defies expectation; it leads to an unpredictable place.

The path of wisdom

I'd venture that it is a mark of wisdom to believe in God. What makes it wise is our simple proposition that faith makes life better. Everyone wants to be happy. In the Indian tradition, you can choose two paths to happiness. One is the path of pleasure; the other, the path of wisdom. The path of pleasure is based upon maximizing all the experiences that feel good and minimizing those that feel bad. Instinctively children follow this path, not by choosing it but by preferring pleasure over pain. The same instincts persist when we grow up. Our brains are wired to react to painful stimuli by storing them in memory as something to avoid in the future. In the most primitive region of the brain, the reptilian brain, basic sensations of pain and pleasure create a strong physical response, which is why we gravitate toward sex, food, and creature comfort.

The path of wisdom must override this basic setup, and we do that all the time. A marathon runner endures pain for the sake of reaching the end of the race. A prudent eater denies herself rich, fatty desserts for the sake of staying healthy. Human beings do not operate on the pleasure principle; we are too complex to be ruled by any simple brain mechanism. But prudent living isn't the same as living wisely. Nor is wisdom found in adages like "Things have a way of working themselves out" or "Time heals all wounds." Wise saws are based on collective experience, which can be helpful. It's mostly true that time heals all wounds and that bad situations, if left alone, tend to work themselves out. But Socrates, the wisest man in Athens, opposed another school of philosophers, the Sophists, because they packaged wisdom and doled it out to their students in neat packages. Socrates held that wisdom could not be taught; in fact, that is its predominant characteristic.

Wisdom is discovered inside a situation; it is elusive and changeable. You cannot confine it to rules and adages. Most of the time wisdom startles us because it is so contrary to reason and common sense. A Buddhist parable makes this point. In ancient India, a disciple hears of a great teacher residing in a cave in remotest Tibet. He sells his worldly goods and makes the arduous journey across the Himalayas to find the cave. After many trials, the disciple arrives at the cave and prostrates himself before the teacher.

"I'm told that you are the wisest of men," the disciple entreats. "Impart your wisdom to me. Show me how to become enlightened."

The teacher is a grumpy old man who resents being disturbed by this intruder. Shaking his head, he replies, "Do you think wisdom is handed out for free? Bring me a bag of gold dust, and if you have brought enough, I will make you enlightened."

Hearing this, the disciple almost loses heart, but he gathers himself up and returns to India, where he toils to fill a bag with gold dust. A long time passes. Then the disciple retraces the arduous journey across the Himalayas and prostrates himself before the teacher.

"I've done as you asked, master. I've filled a bag with gold dust so that you might teach me the way to enlightenment."

The teacher holds out his hand. "Show me."

Trembling, the disciple takes the bag out from under his cloak, the payment for years of slavery. The teacher grabs it and with a toss throws the gold into the air. Within seconds the wind has carried it away.

"What? What?" the disciple cries in dismay.

"I have no use for gold," the teacher says. "I'm old and live in a cave. Don't you know that money cannot buy wisdom?"

The disciple's jaw falls; his head is swimming. Suddenly the teacher takes off his shoe and slaps the disciple hard against the ear. At that instant, the disciple is filled with total clarity. The truth dawns. He has awakened.

Wisdom stories are often like this—they lead to a surprising conclusion because the mind, stuck in its conventional thinking, must be shocked into seeing the light. The Christian version, which is much less dramatic, is condensed into Jesus's teaching in Matthew 19:24, "Again I tell you, it is easier for a camel to go through the eye of a needle than for a rich man to enter the kingdom of God." Both are about a mind that goes beyond worldly concerns. (I've told the Buddhist tale as I heard it, although later I discovered that it's an amalgam of stories told about two illustrious Tibetan masters, Naropa and Milarepa.)

The path of wisdom has been called "the pathless path" just because it has no fixed guidelines. There's no curriculum, and most frustrating of all, a teacher isn't of much help. Mostly the teacher says, "I've been where you are now. Keep going." The rest is taken on faith. If there were another way, frankly, most people would take it. The path of pleasure had to fail before the path of wisdom had a chance. In Buddhism, the seeker cannot take the first step until he or she has given up on pleasure. This bald fact was encapsulated in a doctrine known as the Four Noble Truths, which begins with "Life is suffering." If you unpack this brutal statement, it comes down to the unreliability of pleasure.

There isn't enough pleasure in the world to stave off suffering. Some kinds of pain (such as the death of a child or killing someone by accident) cannot be healed with extra doses of pleasure. Guilt and shame make deep, often permanent impressions. The past leaves scars. As if all of that weren't enough, aging and death are inevitable.

But something deeper is at work. The same thing that roots life in suffering also leads to the way out of suffering: self-awareness. We are the only creatures who have awareness that pain is inevitable. We can foresee future pain, and that is enough to remove the savor of present pleasure. Without self-awareness, you can't feel guilty about the bad things you've done or past wounds that remind you of your failings. (As one mordant wit remarked, "I don't want to come back after I die if it means going through junior high school again.")

Self-awareness plunges us into the sad knowledge that we were born to suffer. But at the same time it offers a solution: the path of wisdom. Why was the disciple suddenly enlightened when his teacher hit him on the head with his shoe? The act itself wasn't the reason. Rather, he had a stroke of self-awareness, in which he realized that being in the world—working, raising a family, learning how to do all the right things—takes place at a different level from the truth. Of course the parable is simplistic. In real life, learning how to obey Christ's injunction to "be in the world but not of it" takes years. Wisdom is a process of inner growth; it doesn't come about instantly.

Once you accept that life is suffering, the other three Noble Truths follow:

Suffering is caused by attachment.
There's a way to bring suffering to an end.
The path for ending suffering has eight necessary parts to it.

The eight necessary parts (formally known as the Eightfold Path) are joined together by the word *right*: right view, right intention, right speech, right action, right livelihood, right effort, right mindfulness, and right concentration. Leaving aside some terminology that is specifically Buddhist, such as *mindfulness,* the core issue comes down to a single question: What does *right* mean? Unfortunately, no simple answer emerges. Buddha didn't provide a playbook for the game of life. His version of wisdom, like every other, cannot be reduced to a formula with fixed rules.

I realize that for many Buddhists, as for many Christians, the teaching of wisdom winds up in some impossible contradictions. (You can work so hard at being good to others, for example, that you stop being good to yourself.) This is a major problem. When you look closely at Jesus's teaching about turning the other cheek, it's no wonder that very few Christians manage to follow it.

> "But I tell you, do not resist an evil person. If someone strikes you on the right cheek, turn to him the other also. And if someone wants to sue you and take your tunic, let him have your cloak as well. If someone forces you to go one mile, go with him two miles." (Matthew 5:39–41)

This passage from the New Testament falls under the Buddhist category of doing and thinking what is "right," but we continue to ignore "resist not evil," just as Buddhists and Hindus sometimes turn their backs on the doctrine of Ahimsa, which tells them to do no harm to any living creature. The path of wisdom very often defies common sense, human nature, and social practicalities. As a matter of course, we resist evil, punish wrongdoers, and refuse to go the extra mile. It is so counterintuitive to follow wisdom that there are only two choices: Either pay lip service to the great spiritual teachers while living your own life, or reduce their teachings to simple rules of morality and conduct.

Neither alternative comes close to the intention of a Christ or a Buddha. They were not moralists. They were radicals who showed the way to inner transformation. I'm not condemning practicing Christians as failures when they resist evil instead of turning the other cheek. It isn't a failing, either, that Buddhists reduce the Eightfold Path to an admirable cut-and-dried set of ethics. Human beings can always use reminders to be peaceful, treat other people decently, and act out of love instead of anger. By comparison, a teaching that would completely overturn everyday behavior seems more threatening than healing. So let me take a moment to defend the path of wisdom in all its radicalism. Since the Christian message is so well known (and has been temporarily discredited by right-wing fundamentalists), I'll use Buddha and his solution for suffering instead.

Doctor Buddha

Looking around at the state of the world, we feel overwhelmed by its chaos, which seems to be teetering between madness and catastrophe. Yet when people came to Buddha more than two thousand years ago, they brought the same complaints as ours. They felt helpless in the face of natural disasters, war, and poverty. They couldn't comprehend a world on the edge of madness.

When I was young, a few seminal ideas guided my life. One of them (now well known in the West) was expressed by Mahatma Gandhi: "Be the change that you want to see in the world." Because the world is so huge, it came as a revelation to me—and also a mystery—that by changing myself I could affect the world. The idea wasn't original with Gandhi. It's an offshoot of a much older idea, traceable to ancient Vedic India, which says, "As you are, so is the world." This is the same as saying that the world begins in consciousness. Buddha was famously practical. He told people to stop analyzing the world and its troubles and to stop relying on religious rituals and sacrifices.

By refusing to accept a religious culture that had become rigid and divorced from individual lives, Buddha was the avatar of the situation we find ourselves in today, where God seems disconnected from the individual. Buddha didn't justify the social safety net of the priestly caste with its automatic connection to the invisible world of spirit. Above all, he accepted the inescapable fact that each person is ultimately alone in the world. This aloneness is the very disease Buddha set out to cure.

His cure was a waking-up process, in which suffering came to be seen as rooted in false consciousness, specifically in the dulled awareness that causes us to accept illusion for reality. The steps of waking up have trickled down into the everyday life of practicing Buddhists:

- Meditate on the core of silence within the mind.
- Observe the shifting contents of the mind carefully, separating out anything that sustains suffering and illusion.
- Unravel the ego's version of reality and pierce through the ego's claim that it knows how to live properly.
- Face the truth that everything in nature is impermanent.
- Let go of materialism in both its crude and subtle forms.
- Become detached from the self and realize that the individual self is an illusion.
- Be mindful of one's being; overcome the distraction of thoughts and sensations.
- Abide by a set of higher ethics whose basis is compassion for other people and reverence for life.

Some or all of these things stand for Buddha's path of wisdom, by which the disease of suffering can be cured. So how is the cure proceeding? Let's say that an outsider is coming in from the cold. He or she wants to be free of pain and suffering and wants to feel that life at its core is meaningful. An outsider could think that the Buddhist cure has become difficult, complicated, and confusing. Every aspect has its drawbacks:

- Sitting and trying to find a core of silence is beyond the average person's short attention span and doesn't fit into the hectic pace of modern life.
- Watching and examining the shifting contents of the mind is time-consuming and exhausting.
- Confronting the ego is nearly impossible, because it has a hundred heads for every one you cut off.
- Facing the truth that everything is impermanent frightens people.
- Seeking detachment makes people think they will be giving up worldly success and comfort.
- Abiding by a set of higher ethics makes people anxious that they will be prey to anyone who is stronger, less moral, and capable of using violence without any sense of guilt or remorse.

Even if you believe that these objections are unfair to Buddhism, bringing wisdom to a world built on illusion and suffering is difficult. Solving violence through pacifism is unworkable. Detaching from materialism has little appeal when people everywhere are rabid consumers of material goods. Yet the genius of Buddha's teaching lies in its universality, and whatever is universal is also simple enough for everyone to understand.

Right now Buddha's cure isn't simple, because we fear being alone. By asking people to go inside, Buddhism seems to be asking them to be more alone. We are also asked to strip ourselves of labels. Labels fit things you already see before you, things you already know. They work for Jell-O and Chryslers but not for invisible things. *Soul* and *God* are therefore false labels. So is the self, which is tagged with misleading labels of all kinds. I can label myself an Indian male, a husband and father, a breadwinner, a citizen, and so on. All these are things I see and know already.

Can I label my inner self the same way? No. To Buddha, God and the soul were question marks, because the seeker after God doesn't even know who "I" am. Nothing is closer to each of us than our sense of self, but if it remains a mystery, what good does it do us to pursue higher mysteries? Someone who seeks solace from God and communion with the soul has turned them into spiritual security blankets. There is no comfort in the unknown, and it is pure wish fulfillment to think of God as anything but unknown—so Buddha taught.

He was a master diagnostician of spiritual afflictions; he understood that when people prayed to the Hindu gods, they were praying to creations of the mind, and that what the mind creates has no lasting truth. Maybe a person can be clever enough to disguise his ego while projecting it as an all-powerful, all-knowing, all-present deity. But whenever the known is projected into the unknown, something false is happening, and the truth moves further away. Wisdom is a great respecter of the unknown. It isn't distracted by the mind's incessant need to create pleasing illusions.

Buddha was a radical surgeon, cutting out all labels that put a name on the unknown. Naturally, people who came to him for comfort and solace were shocked that he proposed major surgery. They saw themselves as humble seekers after truth, which they would hear from his lips. Buddha knew better than to satisfy them—instead, he overturned their expectations about how truth works.

Truth isn't found in words but through insight and self-discovery.

Truth isn't taught or learned. It is wrapped inside consciousness itself.

Your consciousness must deepen until what is false has been left behind. Then truth will exist by itself, strong and self-sufficient.

These are universal statements applicable to everyone's life. Yet Buddha's teaching became easy prey for the ego-personality. Let's say that you are being true to your higher self—or God or the soul—by practicing Ahimsa, the doctrine of nonviolence and reverence for life that one finds in every Eastern tradition. And not just there. The Hippocratic Oath taken by physicians, which begins "First, do no harm," is an expression of Ahimsa. But Ahimsa can easily turn out to be part of the human disease rather than the cure. Following where nonviolence leads, I may become a pacifist who finds himself hated by his country for refusing to protect it from enemies. This hatred may lead to persecution, and so I become a martyr to the truth. I get thrown in jail—or *in extremis* I become a monk setting himself on fire in Vietnam to stir the conscience of the world—and in the end I suffer more than if I hadn't learned this truth called Ahimsa.

The web of the ego is complicated, and the negative possibilities I've mentioned have marred the good intent of Ahimsa when it was put into practice. I could pick another spiritual value instead, like love. People have killed in the name of love and suffered terribly in countless ways. The positive is always woven in with the negative. Truth can cause suffering; it can deepen the illusions of the separate self. Does the good of nonviolence outweigh the bad? After all, peaceful disobedience freed India under Gandhi and led to civil rights reform in the racist South under Martin Luther King, Jr., an avowed follower of Gandhi's principles. Buddha didn't measure truth that way. If it were enough to tell people to go and cause no harm, the human disease wouldn't need a drastic cure.

Inner revolution

Buddha wanted to pluck out the seed of illusion, not to feed the mind with new ideals that would succumb to corruption. He aimed for nothing less than an inner revolution. I think inner revolution is the purest form and the highest purpose of wisdom, as stated in the original Buddhist teachings, the Theravada, whose aim was to make people not into Buddhists but into Buddhas.

Coming in from the cold, modern people yearn for some kind of inner transformation because there is a hole inside them where God used to be. Buddha's radical cure is necessary when nothing less will do. Filling the hole with a new image of God merely replaces one illusion with another. Some people would disagree. In Mahayana, the "greater way" of Buddhism, personal enlightenment came to be seen as selfish. For me to try to become enlightened in a suffering world isn't morally right. A different goal—compassion for all living things—arose as a substitute ideal. Mahayana Buddhism stands for healing the suffering we see all around us. One lifetime after another, each Bodhisattva (awakened person) is offered the choice between personal enlightenment (i.e., saving himself) and service to humanity (i.e., postponing personal salvation). Always, they choose the latter. This is altruism that never ends—realistically, the world cannot be saved by a handful of enlightened beings, though it can be strongly influenced.

My mind comes back to practicalities. I can't settle centuries-old disputes among deep religious thinkers. The value of inner transformation doesn't depend on Buddhism and right doctrine. The same promise was held out by the Vedic sages who lived long before Buddha; by Socrates, who was born soon after Buddha died; and by Jesus five hundred years later. Each opened up the pathless path using different words. When you reach higher consciousness by any means, you no longer separate what is good for you from what is good for everyone. Humanity contains Buddha nature (the source of compassion); the world contains Buddha nature; the cosmos is nothing but Buddha nature.

The reason that the average person cannot live the pure teachings of Jesus or Buddha is that these teachings depend upon higher consciousness. Otherwise, turning the other cheek will get you beaten up twice as badly. Burning yourself up to protest the Vietnam War will be an act of futile pain. Even devoting yourself to sick, orphaned babies in Calcutta might bring painful disillusionment. Most of the time, in fact, the teaching of wisdom can't be applied effectively to the surface of life.

An inner revolution must occur along the way. By finding a new level of awareness, one solves the negatives of Buddha's radical cure—isolation, fear of detachment, anxiety about becoming weak and passive, the apprehension that nirvana will be cosmic loneliness.

To me, the Eightfold Path represents a way to find out who you really are by inviting your awareness to show what *it* really is. Many practicing Buddhists strive for right action, right speech, or right thought because they are virtues spouted by an enlightened person. I think there's a better reason. These values are innate. They are part of every person's makeup once we drop our disguises. I mentioned Ahimsa to show that it has hidden pitfalls. Those pitfalls exist if you struggle to be nonviolent, if you suppress your anger and resentment, disciplining yourself with gritted teeth to meet evil with good. At bottom you are still judging against yourself for harboring the seed of violence, and self-judgment is the root of guilt and shame. How can reminding yourself to be kind ever turn into spontaneous kindness? The mystery of Buddha's cure is this: What you seek you already are.

If people could see that the human disease is temporary, a station on the way to enlightenment, I think wisdom would speak to the world's problems in very real ways. Wisdom could guide trends that are already moving ahead. We are already becoming more peaceful, for example. In the past forty years more than eighty dictators have fallen. Deaths from large-scale conflicts, including civil wars, have drastically decreased. Even broader trends are moving in the right direction. In America, the past decade has seen declines in abortion, teenage pregnancy, drug use among the young, and overall violent crime. Wisdom tells us to nurture and guide these trends if we can.

If you need somewhere to put your faith, look to the agenda of wisdom, which is based on rising consciousness. The blueprint of the future is invisible, but something important is working its way through the global mind.

If Wisdom Has Its Way

A future based on raising consciousness

Meditation will become mainstream.

Natural ways of healing, both physical and psychological, will become commonplace.

Prayer will be seen as real and efficacious.

Manifestation of desires will be talked about as a real phenomenon.

People will regain a connection to spirit. Individuals will find answers inwardly to their deepest spiritual questions. They will believe in their private answers and live accordingly.

Communities of belief will arise.

Spiritual authorities will wane in influence.

A wisdom tradition will grow to embrace the great spiritual teachings at the heart of every religion.

Faith will no longer be seen as an irrational departure from reason and science.

Wars will decline as peace becomes a social reality.

Nature will regain its sacred value.

These may seem like baby steps compared to Buddha's deep teaching of enlightenment or Jesus's universal love. I feel just the opposite. Every step forward contains a hint of Buddha nature. If you notice these hints and give them value, they will expand, and in time they will fill the hole of lonely isolation and the threat of meaninglessness. The path of wisdom is natural and open to everyone. Einstein said as much when he considered how God relates to everyday life: "Whatever there is of God in the universe, it must work itself out and express itself through us." In a sentence Einstein outlined the agenda of wisdom. Wisdom is the divine working itself out and expressing itself through us.

Wisdom tells us secrets before we have a right to know them. That's the beauty of it. You don't have to pray for wisdom or make yourself worthy of it. As with the concept of grace in the New Testament, which falls like rain on the just and the unjust alike, the ultimate truth simply *is*. When we catch a glimpse of it, we become more real in ourselves. It is undeniable that the outward appearance of life contains suffering and distress. Wisdom reveals that suffering comes and goes while a deeper reality never changes. That reality is founded on truth and love.

Faith makes life better because in the midst of pain and suffering, we need to trust that something else is more powerful. Your present self, in its unawakened state, isn't your enemy or a cripple or a failure. It is Buddha waiting to realize itself. It's the seed of wisdom needing to be nurtured.

Are Miracles Possible?

Miracles are a joyous release from everything we expect is possible. But they lay a trap for both sides of the God debate. For believers, if miracles aren't real, then God might not be real either. For unbelievers, the trap is just the opposite: If a single miracle can be proven to have happened, then the door is open for God. It might seem easy enough to validate a miracle and agree that it was real—such effort has been going on for centuries. But there can be no common ground when both sides are deaf to each other's arguments. Atheists are unconvinced by any amount of eyewitness testimony to a miracle. They deem fake all apparitions of the Virgin Mary, of which there are hundreds. They regard all faith healing as mere coincidence; the patient was about to recover anyway. They think psychic powers have no basis in fact, despite numerous controlled studies to prove that they exist.

One advantage of coming from India is that it remains a faith-based society, untouched in many regions by the inroads of modernism. A boy growing up in such a setting could easily accept that supernatural occurrences were not deviations from reality. They were part of the landscape where God seeped into every nook and crevice. One heard of holy men and women, for instance, who never ate food or drank water. Their devotees claimed to have kept close watch for years, even decades, without seeing any food pass the holy man's mouth. For two weeks in 2010, a branch of the Indian defense department put a yogi named Prahlad Jani under hospital observation with round-the-clock attendants and closed-circuit television. Jani ate and drank nothing during that time and showed no changes in his vital signs or metabolism. A team of thirty-five researchers took part in the trial, so the possibility of collusion or fakery was basically nonexistent.

Jani, who tested medically like someone half his age, was eighty-three and lived in a temple; his devotees said that he hadn't eaten for seventy years. Skeptics dismissed the results on various grounds. Some pointed out that Jani was allowed to gargle and bathe, which gave him access to water. Others noted that he left the sealed room to sunbathe, and that devotees were occasionally given access. Since the results of the test were medically "impossible," some form of cheating must have taken place.

When such an episode is transposed from a society steeped in faith to a society steeped in science, almost no reaction is possible except disbelief. Yet in the West cases of the same kind have been documented. In the eighteenth century, a Scottish girl named Janet McLeod lived for four years without eating. A detailed report was submitted to the Royal Society in London in 1767 attesting to the reality of the case. While the Catholic Church has amassed its own records of saintly people who lived without eating or drinking, in other cases, such as Janet McLeod's, there was no spiritual connection. In fact, she was deemed seriously ill.

Even if you find the evidence compelling, what causes such an extraordinary phenomenon? When the few individuals who have totally stopped eating are asked for an explanation, they don't agree. Some stopped as an act of faith; others spontaneously began to live, they say, on sunlight or the life-force (prana). A handful quit eating as the result of illness, while a modern group calling themselves Breatharians believe that the most natural way to gain nourishment is through the air we breathe.

Beginning with "impossible"

Strong skeptics accept none of these accounts as anything but fraudulent or delusional. In his 2011 book for young readers, *The Magic of Reality*, Richard Dawkins devotes a chapter to miracles, which, as one would expect, he approaches with a mixture of strict rationality and debunking fervor. The purpose of the book, as encapsulated in its subtitle, is to instruct its readers in "How we know what's really true." Dawkins's agenda is given away by the cautionary word *really*, implying that there are ways of knowing the truth that might seem valid but aren't.

Miracles serve as an object lesson in every frailty of belief, from mass hysteria to hallucination. Methodically Dawkins tells us that any number of miracles are the tricks of stage magicians working in front of credulous audiences. At other times eyewitnesses are so primitive and childlike that natural phenomena awe them, as in the famous "cargo cults" that arose on the islands around New Guinea after World War II. The islanders had looked on as Japanese and Allied airplanes landed, unloading huge amounts of war supplies. They had never seen airplanes before, and the sudden influx of material goods seemed to be a gift from the gods. When the foreigners disappeared after 1945, the islanders appealed to their gods to bring back the "cargo," the material goods that had flowed in abundance. To entice the gods, the islanders built crude replicas of airstrips and planes. A supernatural significance was attached to events that seem completely natural to us.

Dawkins's skepticism about miracles is certainly defensible. It's possible, as he argues, that the miracles recorded in the New Testament are just as unreliable as modern-day miracles but have acquired legitimacy simply through the passage of time. (Dawkins can't control his tendency to insinuate bad motives, so he cheerfully tells young readers that miracles are generally associated with charlatans, implicitly including

Jesus and the disciples.) But I imagine his unsophisticated readership won't spot the weakness of Dawkins's "proof" that miracles don't exist. Once more he relies on probabilities, just as he does with God. He proposes that if any other explanation is more probable than a true miracle, one must accept the alternative explanation.

He prominently cites the "Miracle of the Sun" witnessed by numerous people gathered in an open field near Fatima, Portugal, on October 13, 1917. Thousands were assembled (the estimate varies widely, from 3,000 to 400,000) because three young shepherd children had predicted that the Virgin Mary would appear at noon that day. For the children, who had already had visions of her, the prediction came true. They reported seeing Mary, Jesus, and other holy apparitions. What many eyewitnesses saw was something different but equally inexplicable.

The day had been gray and rainy, soaking the ground and the expectant spectators. All at once the clouds parted, and the sun showed itself, not in its usual brightness but as a dark, opaque orb. It radiated multicolored beams across the sky and on the whole landscape. Then the sun zigzagged its way closer to Earth, making some terrified observers believe that Judgment Day had arrived. After ten minutes the phenomenon was over, and as reported by local journalists, many witnesses attested that their clothing and the muddy ground had become completely dry. After extensive examination, the Catholic Church recognized the genuineness of the miracle in 1930.

Dawkins cannot prove that such events didn't occur. His task is simply to state definitively that they are impossible and then argue his way back from there. The problem is that "impossible" is the very assumption that miracles disprove (should they be real). To cover this weakness, Dawkins falls back on probability, telling the young reader to consider two possibilities. A: The sun behaves the way astronomy says it behaves. B: The sun jumps around the sky and does crazy things the way the eyewitnesses at Fatima claim. Which is more likely? A sane, rational person must pick A, the view of science. He makes a more extended presentation than this, to the point of reducing astronomy to baby talk, but the gaping hole hasn't been filled. Miracles defy science; they don't contradict it. Astronomy can be right 99.9999 percent of the time. That doesn't disprove miracles, and by the same token, the miracle of the sun doesn't disprove astronomy.

The whole thing is an inescapable conundrum. *Something* has been intruding into everyday existence that must be explained. History was once on the side of miracles, which were accepted without question. Now skepticism is accepted without question. Thus miracles are a vexing problem when we try to straighten out the muddle surrounding God. Do they have to be real for God to be real?

No. When Thomas Jefferson edited his own version of the New Testament, he deleted the miracles while retaining his faith. Among the four gospels, the Book of John tells Jesus's story without mentioning miracles, not even the virgin birth and the Christmas story. One has to be clear that every faith contains denominations that accept God without accepting miracles. But skeptics use *supernatural* as a buzzword for ignorant credulity. In his chapter on "the tawdriness of the miraculous," Christopher Hitchens scoffs that "the age of miracles seems to lie somewhere in the past. If the religious were wise, or had the confidence of their convictions, they ought to welcome the eclipse of this age of fraud and conjuring."

Most miracles, however, do not have a star player who offers amazing tricks. Jesus was an exception. More common was the appearance of the Virgin Mary in the hardscrabble village of Knock in Western Ireland in 1879. Two women walking in the rain saw an illuminated tableau that replaced the back wall of the local church. They summoned thirteen other people, who attested to seeing the vision over the next two hours, when Mary appeared in white robes and a gold crown, her hands raised in prayer. She was flanked by Saint Joseph and John the Evangelist; before them was an altar circled by angels. The spectators ranged in age from five to seventy-five. They were strictly examined for truthfulness by the Church that same year and again in 1936. Other villagers who didn't rush to the scene described seeing bright light emanating from the locality of the church, and several healings occurred in the vicinity. There was no possibility of a stage illusionist, in any case. One can choose to shrug off the event as a fraud, mass delusion, or a phenomenon awaiting explanation. Without a doubt, however, all believed in what they saw.

Hitchens is obviously wrong to label miracles petty and tawdry. Still, it's undeniable that religion brings the supernatural down to earth, so to speak, from its home in another, invisible dimension. Saint Augustine declared, "I would not be a Christian except for the miracles." The onus is on believers in miracles—they must show that miracles can exist peaceably beside reason, logic, and science. We've already seen the limitations of choplogic, reason mixed with prejudice, and pseudoscience. Skeptics can't disprove miracles, so they cut corners to provide a show of proof. Faith has a stronger position, and not merely by amassing eyewitness accounts of miraculous healing that extend even to the present day. Faith sees the divine in every aspect of creation. All the world's wisdom traditions declare that there is only one reality, which embraces any conceivable phenomenon. If miracles have any chance, they must fit into reality as securely as planets, trees, DNA, and the law of gravity.

A scientist sees a healing

Establishing that miracles exist requires two steps. First, we have to take down the wall that separates the natural from the supernatural. Fortunately, that's fairly easy to do since the wall was artificial to begin with. The basis of everything in the physical world is the quantum domain. If anything deserves to be called the zone of miracles, it is this level of nature. Here the laws that make miracles "impossible" are fluid. The constraints of space and time as we know them do not hold.

One of the most revered among modern Catholic saints was a humble southern Italian priest, Padre Pio (1887–1968), who caused consternation in the Church by gathering huge crowds and countless believers among the common people. Besides healing the sick, one of Padre Pio's miracles was bilocation, appearing in two places at once. If this occurrence happened at the quantum level, miracles would be a simple matter. Every particle in the universe can also transition into the state of a wave embedded in the quantum field, and instead of existing in two places at once, such waves exist everywhere at once.

But Padre Pio wasn't a quantum; therefore the behavior common to the subtlest level of nature can't automatically be transferred to the grosser level where we live our lives. There must be a second step of proof, showing that the merging of natural and supernatural takes place all around us. Skeptics consider this step impossible, but that's far from the case. Scientists have been present for supernatural events. There have been hundreds of controlled experiments in psychic phenomena, for example. When a scientist views an actual miracle, however, the inner conflict that results is acute.

In May 1902 a young French physician named Alexis Carrel boarded a train bound for Lourdes. A friend, another doctor, had asked him to be in attendance on a group of the sick who were traveling to the famous shrine in hopes of a cure. Normally the dying were not permitted on board, but a woman named Marie Bailly had smuggled herself on. She was dying of complications from tuberculosis, the disease that had killed both her parents. Her belly was hard and distended from peritonitis; doctors in Lyon had refused to operate given the severe risk that she would die during surgery.

During the trip Carrel was called to Bailly's side when the woman became semiconscious. He examined her, confirmed the diagnosis of tubercular peritonitis, and predicted that she would die before reaching Lourdes. But Bailly regained consciousness, and when she insisted, against medical advice, on being carried to the healing pools, Carrel accompanied her. The reader will have no trouble anticipating that I am about to recount a miraculous healing—Dossier 54, the official medical records of Marie Bailly's case, are among the most famous in Lourdes history. But the presence of Dr. Carrel makes the tale far more enigmatic.

Bailly was carried on a stretcher to the pools but was too fragile to be immersed in the waters. She was in her mid-twenties and had already survived a bout of meningitis brought on by her TB, which she attributed to Lourdes water. Now she insisted that a pitcher of the pool's water be poured over her swollen abdomen. Carrel, who was an assistant professor in the anatomy department of the medical faculty in Lyon, stood behind her stretcher taking notes. When the water was poured over her abdomen, which was covered by a blanket, Bailly felt hot pain, but she asked for a second application, which was less painful, and then a third, which gave her a pleasant sensation.

Over the next half hour, her distended abdomen shrank under the blanket until it became completely flat. No discharge was seen from the body. Carrel examined the patient. The hard mucinous mass that he had detected on the train was completely gone. Within a few days Bailly rode back to Lyon to tell her family about the miracle. She joined a charitable Catholic order that cared for the sick and died in 1937 at the age of fifty-eight. A medical exam in the aftermath of her recovery revealed that Bailly had no signs of tuberculosis; she passed all physical and mental tests.

For all the hundreds of thousands of visitors to Lourdes, the number of confirmed healings accredited by its medical bureau is scanty. In Bailly's case, two other physicians besides Carrel attested to her cure, but the Church eventually rejected the case as miraculous in 1964. They cited as their reason that the attending physicians had not considered the possibility of pseudoscyesis, or false pregnancy. Skeptics have leaped on that diagnosis, even though false pregnancies do not reveal hard masses in the abdomen when a physician palpates it; it is also unlikely that Bailly would have convinced a number of physicians that she was dying if she wasn't, or that her belly could have flattened in half an hour without discharge.

But it's Alexis Carrel who fascinates me, since he serves as a proxy for the inner struggle we experience between faith and reason. Having witnessed the healing firsthand, Carrel returned to Lyon with no desire to publicize the event. The University of Lyon was strongly anticlerical in the medical department. Unfortunately for him, a local newspaper carried a story about Bailly's healing, which became a sensation. Carrel was mentioned as one of the witnesses, and he was forced to come forward with an account. He tried his best to hedge, declaring that what he saw was real but must have some unknown natural cause. But fence-sitting did him no good. When the medical faculty got the news, a senior professor told him, "It's useless to insist, sir, that with views such as these you can ever be received as a member of our faculty. We have no place for you here."

Unable to secure a hospital appointment, Carrel emigrated to Canada, then to the United States, where he joined the newly established Rockefeller Institute for Medical Research in 1906. He remained intrigued by what he had seen but was not a believer in miracles—he had been brought up in a devout family and educated by the Jesuits but was no longer a practicing Catholic by the time he became a physician. Another event, fortuitous for him rather than miraculous, had shaped his career. In 1894, when Carrel was a young surgeon, the president of France, Sadi Carnot, had been stabbed in the abdomen with a knife by an assassin. A large abdominal vein was severed, and there was no reliable surgical technique for suturing large blood vessels. Carnot lingered and died two days later.

Carrel was then motivated to study the anatomy of blood vessels and the way they connect naturally or through surgery. For his work he was awarded the Nobel Prize in medicine in 1912. Upon returning to France, he followed up on his fascination with Bailly's healing, returning to Lourdes repeatedly on the chance that he might observe another possible miracle and find a natural explanation. In 1910 he witnessed an eighteen-month-old infant suddenly regain its sight after being born blind. But he never satisfactorily resolved his perplexity. After the publication in France of his memoir, *The Voyage to Lourdes,* in 1948, four years after his death, Carrel became controversial: *Scientific American* published a skeptical article in 1994 (which also covered, with admiration, his work with blood vessels), yet he was hotly defended among the Catholic faithful.

Where do miracles belong in regaining one's faith? They would appear to be a prime example of "what you believe, you see." The faithful are primed to accept miracles; skeptics are primed to reject them out of hand. This may seem obvious, but we can go deeper. If factors hidden inside your mind dictate your perception, then the whole issue of searching for rock-solid evidence may be a red herring.

The real issue is how to unite the natural and the supernatural, just as Dr. Carrel wanted to do. Separating the two is merely a habit. Science is made to fit inside one mental box, miracles inside another. The time has passed when the boxes have to be kept sealed. I want to show that you don't have to abolish miracles to have science—quite the opposite. When Einstein said that a sense of awe and wonder was necessary for any great scientific discovery, he wasn't being soft-minded. In a universe where visible matter accounts for only 0.01 percent of creation, it would be foolish to undertake science without a sense that reality is extremely mysterious. Dark energy exists on the fringe of the unknowable, and so does a saint who exists without eating. The simplistic logic and outmoded science applied by Dawkins and company don't remotely approach how reality works.

In 1905 Pope Pius X declared that rigorous medical investigations must be conducted at Lourdes before any healing could be confirmed as miraculous. To date, after extensive critical review, sixty-seven cures have been officially confirmed as miracles. The latest, from 2002, is of a Frenchman who was healed of paralysis, an event that twenty physicians at the Lourdes Medical Bureau have labeled "remarkable." That's a considerable distance from miraculous, but do numbers really matter? It would be necessary, not to tot up all the supposed miracles in history, of which there are thousands, but to explain just one. The supernatural has no validity until it can be connected to the natural; a world apart satisfies no one except believers, who are simply the reverse of skeptics, accepting as easily as their opposites reject.

Because there is only one reality, it is continuous. Chopping reality up into slices like a loaf of bread makes it more understandable. The slices that taste of the supernatural can be thrown away. Science has made finer and finer cuts, getting near the very source of matter and energy. But if you claim that bread comes only in slices, denying the whole loaf, you've made a mistake. The analogy may be humble, but this is the mistake made by modern science: It has brilliantly subdivided nature into tiny packets of knowledge while missing the miraculousness of the whole.

Natural/Supernatural

The healing of Marie Bailly may seem like a supernatural event, but it was surrounded by everyday occurrences. Her sickness had proceeded normally. It was about to follow a natural course that ends in death. Then suddenly, without apparent cause, the seams of everyday existence came apart. What possible explanation begins to make sense of it? A hint of the answer was provided decades ago by one of the most brilliant quantum pioneers, Wolfgang Pauli, when he said, "It is my personal opinion that in the science of the future reality will neither be 'psychic' nor 'physical' but somehow both and somehow neither." By using a word that science shuns—*psychic*—Pauli was pointing to a kind of ultimate mystery.

The vast physical mechanism we call the universe behaves more like a mind than like a machine. How did mind ever find a way to manifest as the physical world? That question brings us to the merging of the natural and the supernatural, because the very fact that *anything* exists is supernatural—literally beyond the rules of the natural world.

Supernatural Events, Here and Now

Beyond all rules and explanations

- No one can show at what point simple molecules, like the glucose in the brain, become conscious. Does blood sugar "think" when it enters the brain? It doesn't think in a test tube. What makes the difference?

- Tissues automatically heal when they are injured or invaded by disease organisms. The healing system spontaneously assesses the damage and brings the exact repairs needed. It defies explanation that a machine could learn how to repair itself. The laws of nature should dictate that physical breakdown is permanent: Cars don't inflate their punctured tires. Damaged organisms, if they are subject to the same physical laws, should stay damaged—but some kind of X factor has changed that.

- Ever since the Big Bang, the energy in the universe has been dissipating, like a hot stove cooling off. This dispersal of heat, known as entropy, is inexorable. Yet somehow islands of "negative entropy" have evolved. One of them is life on Earth. Instead of dissipating into the void of outer space, the sunlight that hits green plants begins the chain of life, holding on to energy and converting it into incredibly complex forms that hand the energy around, recycle it, and use it in creative ways. It is impossible for random events to explain how entropy could be defied for billions of years.

- DNA was born in a hostile environment filled with extreme heat and cold, toxic gases, and a firestorm of random chemical reactions. Unlike any chemical in the known universe, DNA resisted being degraded into smaller molecules; instead it built itself up into higher complexity and learned to replicate itself. No explanation for this unique activity has been offered.

- All the cells in our bodies, trillions of them, contain the same DNA, yet they spontaneously "know" how to become liver cells, heart cells, and all other specialized cells. In the embryonic brain, stem cells travel along precise paths, stop when they reach their destination, and become specific neurons for seeing, hearing, controlling hormones, and thinking. This spontaneous ability to "know" how to suppress one part of the genetic code while enlivening others is inexplicable.

- DNA can tell time. From the moment an ovum gets fertilized, a single cell contains time-sensitive triggers for growing baby teeth, entering puberty, causing menopause, and eventually dying. How all these sequences, which span seven decades or more, can be contained inside a chemical is beyond explanation.

These mysteries—I've selected a mere handful out of many—cry out for explanation. We mustn't lose sight of what they have in common: They all defy the separation between natural and supernatural. If you aren't wedded to materialism, then you will recognize that there is a common link between islands of negative entropy, embryonic brain cells traveling to their final home, blood sugar learning to think, and the rest. Intelligence is at work. In an uncanny way, molecules "know" what they are doing, whether in the ancestral chemical soup from which DNA emerged or in the chemistry of your brain cells as you read this sentence.

This implies a completely radical view of where the mind began and where it resides. The founder of quantum physics, Max Planck, had no doubt that mind would eventually become the elephant in the room, an issue too massive and obvious to ignore. Planck is worth quoting in full:

> I regard consciousness as fundamental. I regard matter as derivative from consciousness. We cannot get behind consciousness. Everything that we talk about, everything that we regard as existing, postulates consciousness.

If mind is everywhere, we've taken a huge step toward merging the natural and the supernatural. When a person like Marie Bailly is selected to be healed, that's an act of intelligence, no matter how hidden its motives may be, and once the decision is made, the molecules in her body act as if directed—a natural miracle. The healing system we all depend upon, when we cut a finger or come down with the flu, turns into a supernatural miracle. Yet neither can be explained. So there is no reason, in theory, why the intelligence that guides immune cells to rush to the site of invading bacteria might not rush even more quickly to heal an incurable disease.

In other words, there's a sliding scale for the body's response to disease. Let me sketch in the extremes of that sliding scale, keeping in mind than *not a single phase* can be explained medically, even though one extreme is considered natural and the other miraculous, i.e., supernatural.

The Spectrum of Healing

A patient gets sick and recovers in the expected time, without complications.

Another patient contracts the same disease and recovers much faster or much more slowly than normal.

A patient contracts a life-threatening disease and dies.

Another patient contracts a life-threatening disease and recovers
    with normal medical treatment.
Yet another patient contracts a life-threatening disease and
    recovers without treatment.
Very rarely, a patient contracts a life-threatening disease and
    recovers inexplicably because healing happens too fast to fit
    the medical model.

This wide range of outcomes defies any system of prediction. It is as
quirky as thoughts, moods, and other mental events. Different bodies
"decide" how to respond to the same physical condition.

One of the everyday mysteries that medicine can't explain is control by the host. Every minute you and I inhale millions of microbes,
viruses, allergens, and toxic substances. The vast majority reside in us
harmlessly. Our bodies control them from harming us. But when AIDS
destroys the immune system, the host loses control, and rampant disease breaks out in an autoimmune disorder like rheumatoid arthritis.
The system for protecting the body turns upon it instead. Even an
innocuous condition like hay fever indicates that control by the host has
failed. In all these examples, the breakdown is a breakdown of intelligence. Thus mind is pervasive in every cell and swims invisibly through
the bloodstream.

Consciousness holds the key

The reason that mixing mind with matter disturbs mainstream
doctors, who are trained to be scientific, isn't a secret. Mind rules the
subjective world, which science distrusts, while matter is the basis of
"real" knowledge. Heart patients feel all kinds of pain, pressure, and
strangeness about their condition; an angiogram tells the doctor what's
really going on.

Subjectivity is mistrusted for being fickle, individual, shifting, and prey to all kinds of bias. But this mistrust exhibits a strange prejudice, for the body displays all these qualities. Bodies are fickle and highly individual. They make decisions about getting sick that cannot be explained. Medicine has no idea why someone develops a sudden allergy after years of not being allergic. When your body confronts a single cold virus, unpredictability is at work. (Medicine knows that direct contact with a new cold virus infects people only around one in eight times. Why this is so cannot be explained.)

I'm sure that Planck and Pauli were right to suspect that consciousness is more than a given, and that mind and matter are indissolubly linked. Among physicists, these two were not alone. Mind holds some kind of key to the ultimate nature of reality. Once you admit that this is true, the possibility of miraculous events increases, because the non-miraculous has shifted so much. Natural and supernatural are infused with the same properties of consciousness. It turns out that *supernatural* is the label we apply to things we aren't yet comfortable with. In reality, nature goes to the same source to create a galaxy as we go to think of a rose. The field of consciousness embraces both.

Conscious Creation

What it takes to make anything happen

Intelligence

Intention

Attention

A bridge from mind to matter

An observer

A connection between events "in here" and events "out there"

Everything on this list is built into our awareness. As conscious beings, we use them every day, almost entirely without being aware of what we're doing. If you have a math problem to solve, you can select one aspect—intelligence—and focus it on the problem. If your mind wanders from a task, you can bring in another aspect—intention—to combat your distracted mood. So you have no need to go anywhere outside yourself. You possess everything it takes to make the miraculous live peaceably with the rational. The essential thing is that reality is participatory. Nothing is real for us outside our experience of it, and experience is a conscious creative act.

This sounds strange at first. How am I participating when I see the stars at night? The act feels passive. In fact, seeing the stars—or anything at all—requires having every ingredient on the list:

Intelligence: I know what I am looking at and can think about it. Microbes and plants exist under the same stars but are (presumably) unable to think about them.

Intention: I purposely focus on the stars. I see them in particular, as opposed to a photograph, which indiscriminately depicts all objects without singling any out.

Attention: I consciously focus my mind. If my attention is elsewhere—walking home in the dark, listening to music on my iPod, wondering who is walking up behind me—the stars lose my attention.

A bridge from mind to matter: Experiences can't happen without processing in the brain. How photons of light from the stars turn into a visual image in the mind has never been explained. However, it is undeniable that I am experiencing the stars, so *something* is bridging the purely mental and the physical.

An observer: Without me, an observer, there is no proof that the stars exist. This is why Heisenberg declared that consciousness is something science cannot get behind, or go beyond. We only know that we are here observing the world. What happens when nobody observes it is a mystery.

A connection between events "in here" and events "out there": Quantum theory, as part of the so-called observer effect, holds that observation isn't passive. It causes waves to collapse into particles. Something that is invisible, all-pervasive, and subject to the laws of probability turns into something else that is local, physical, and certain. One interpretation calls the observer effect a small glitch in the mathematics that support quantum mechanics. Another interpretation says that the observer effect operates in the real world. In either case, events "in here" are tied to events "out there."

Have I just done what I accused science of doing: cutting up reality into small slices? In the everyday world, all these ingredients merge and operate together. To participate in seeing the stars—or in seeing the Virgin Mary where a church wall should be—you call upon the same aspects of consciousness. None can be left out. What is more important, science does not understand these aspects of consciousness. Are miracles all in your mind? Yes. Is the everyday world all in your mind? Yes again. Having turned its back on consciousness for several hundred years, science is hardly in a position to say what consciousness can or cannot do. The crude manipulations of science by Dawkins and company are even less credible.

Neither Planck nor Pauli followed up on the mystery they had uncovered. They had no need to, not for a long time. Quantum physics blossomed into the most accurate and mathematically sophisticated model in the history of science. It achieved such precise results that its predictive powers were stunning. As the eminent British physicist Sir Roger Penrose notes, Newton's gravitational theory, as applied to the movement of the solar system, is precise to one part in 10 million. Einstein's theory of relativity improved upon Newton by another factor of 10 million.

As spooky as the domain of quarks and bosons may be, even to trained physicists, it obeys mathematical rules and can be predicted using those same rules. Reality, it cannot be denied, has led science along a very productive path. But leaving consciousness out of the equation was like leaving metaphysics out of cookbooks. You don't need metaphysics to measure cake flour and butter, but the commitment to follow reality wherever it leads can make science very uncomfortable, especially when it's time to overturn some cherished assumptions. That time inevitably arrives, for one simple reason: Reality is always more complicated than the models we use to explain it.

Every experience we have, mental or physical, is a miracle, because we have no way of explaining experience scientifically. We assume that photons give us the experience of form and color, yet photons are formless and colorless. We assume that the vibration of air creates sound, but vibrations are silent outside the brain. We study the receptor sites on the tongue and inside the nose that give rise to taste and smell, yet what takes place at those sites is chemical reactions, not an experience. (What did it taste like for oxygen and hydrogen to bond into a molecule of water? The question is meaningless without an experiencer.)

Materialism, in its conquest of the spiritual worldview, has burdened us with explanations requiring just as much faith as believing in miracles. Faith alone supports the notion that sodium and potassium ions passing through the outer membrane of neurons, in turn setting up electrochemical reactions that span millions of neural networks, create sensations, images, feelings, and thoughts. These are assumptions with no explanation whatsoever. Chemicals are just names we have applied to a mystery. Brain scans are snapshots of activity, telling us nothing about actual experience, just as snapshots of piano keys tell us nothing about the experience of enjoying music. Only consciousness makes experience possible; therefore, as the source of consciousness, God exists outside the domain of data.

The same road that leads to miracles leads to God. We haven't traveled the road yet. We've only made the goal possible. That is the role of faith, to expand the range of possibilities. I am not asking anyone to believe in miracles; still less am I attesting to the miracles amassed by the church. All that the supernatural needed, to escape the ridicule of skeptics, was a level playing field. Nature can accommodate any imaginable event. The next step is to turn the highest possibilities, so long cherished in the human heart, into reality.

THE PATH TO GOD

Stage 3: Knowledge

God Without Borders

very time God falters, he comes back tomorrow. When he returns, he doesn't look the same as before. The faithful have dressed him in new clothes; he's undergone a personality makeover. Looking over our shoulder, we have no difficulty distinguishing Jehovah, whose favorite command is "Smite!" from the God of Christianity, whose favorite command is "Love" (but leaving wiggle room for a good deal of smiting). It's harder to see how God will look in the future, however. Almost every divine attribute has been extracted, like silk threads pulled from a cosmic tapestry until the fabric is bare. What's left after you've tried vengeance, love, and everything in between?

In the West one aspect of God has been ignored, a unique trait that is shared with nothing else in creation. It's not that God sees and knows everything. It's not that he is infinitely loving and all powerful. Religion has tested all those qualities, only to end in disappointment. It's inspirational to read, "The Lord is my shepherd, I shall not want," until the day comes when you have many wants and God does nothing about them. But something has been missed that makes God absolutely unique: He cannot be put into a box. As curious as this sounds, it's the most important thing about God. It holds the clue that will lead us to true knowledge. Quite literally, to find God, you must go outside the box.

There are two kinds of boxes that we put things into. One is physical. If you want to study a horned toad, a quark, or a star, you first isolate it as a physical specimen. Sometimes the box isn't literal. No one can containerize a star. But a star is perceived as a thing, an object that sits alone, ready to be studied. God fits into no such box, although the old Sunday-school image of a patriarch sitting on his throne above the clouds attempts to do that.

The other kind of box is mental. In it we put ideas and concepts. *Freedom* is a concept, and so is *enlightenment.* Even though they aren't physical, we still set ideas aside to think about them. A very broad concept that applies to everyone on Earth, such as *human nature,* still fits into a box, ready to be studied like a star or a quark. It doesn't matter that human nature is invisible and very tricky to define. It has to have boundaries that make it different from, say, Buddha nature or the nature of a wolf—the boundaries are its box.

God has no boundaries, however—not if he is omnipresent, which means "everywhere at once." (*He* falsely puts God into a box labeled "masculine," so it's worth repeating that we're using a gender only for the sake of convenience.) Trying to think about him means trying to think about everything at once, which is clearly impossible. People try to get around this impossibility by breaking down God into smaller parts, the way a mechanic breaks down a car engine or a biologist a heart cell. But what works with car engines and brain cells doesn't work with God. Let's say you want to talk about God's love, which people often do. "God's love is eternal and infinite. When I get to heaven, I will bask in his eternal love": This is a religious sentiment that millions of people might say and hope is true. But in fact the words have no meaning.

Infinite is being used to mean "very, very big," but infinity cannot be conceived of that way. Our minds think in finite terms. We look around and see that everything in nature has a beginning and an end. Infinity doesn't. It lies outside our ability to count; it is incompatible with how our minds work in linear time. The only practical use for the word *infinite* is to denote an abstract mathematical concept. We can't meaningfully say that God is very, very big when size doesn't apply to him.

Eternal is being used in the sentence to mean "a very long time." But eternity isn't linear the way that hours, days, and years are. Eternity is infinity applied to time. Therefore the same objection that makes infinity inconceivable applies to eternity. The mind can't wrap itself around time without beginning or end. We can't meaningfully say that God has been around a long, long time when time itself doesn't apply to him.

Love is being used to mean the kind of deep affection and caring that is human love. But God's love doesn't pick and choose, so it applies to serial killers, Adolf Hitler, Chairman Mao, and all other monsters in history. It applies to all criminal acts as well as to holy acts. Therefore divine love is more like a natural force field—gravity, for instance—than a human emotion. Such love can't be expressed into human emotional terms.

I didn't pick a trick sentence here but a fairly typical one. Nor was the wording sloppy, needing a copy editor's red pencil to fix it. *Infinite, eternal,* and *love* simply aren't the right words. They force God into a mental box where he won't fit. There is nothing to be done about it. Yet the journey to know God begins where words fail us. We can ditch the scriptures, sermons, and inspirational writings that have failed us. Faith brought us to a level playing field where God is a real possibility. Beyond faith lie experiences that cannot be put into words. Yet the path is real, and the ability to make the journey is imprinted in the human mind itself.

What cannot be thought

The journey has already begun by acknowledging that it is impossible to think about God the way we think about everything else. If we can't think about him, we can't talk about him, either. As the Vedic seers of India declared, "Those who speak of it know it not. Those who know it, speak of it not." Like a cosmic Houdini, God will escape every kind of box, including all the ones we depend upon the most: time, space, feelings, ideas, and concepts. Hence the mystery.

All the thinking and talking about God that we do is symbolic; thankfully symbols can point the way. The New Testament reaches to find words for God's true nature: "I am Alpha and Omega, the beginning and the end, the first and the last" (Revelation 22:13). More concretely, God has been compared to a calm, still ocean, from which all created things arise like waves. Another symbol is light, by which all things can be seen even though it is invisible. It would be much more convenient if he could be described without symbols. Unfortunately, religion cannot exist without symbols, labels, and categories. When Dawkins and company attack God, they are actually attacking symbols and concepts, which results in a great mass of hot air but nothing with a firm foundation in reality. In India yogis bypass words, seeking to be united with God through deep experience, and once they have achieved divine union, religion no longer applies to them. Being with God sets you free from all restrictions, including religion itself.

In an Indian parable, a holy man chooses the reclusive life. He finds a remote mountain cave and lives there for years in continual meditation. Finally the day comes when he reaches enlightenment. Overjoyed, the holy man rushes down the mountain to tell the local villagers about his liberation. He reaches the town bazaar, which is packed, and begins to make his way through the teeming crowd. Bodies press against his, and an elbow jabs him in the ribs.

"Get out of my way, you idiot," the holy man grumbles. He pauses for a moment, then turns around and heads back up the mountain.

Getting angry when a stranger bumps you in a crowd shows that you aren't enlightened. More than that, the parable is about our need to identify with all kinds of things—emotions, desires, possessions, money, status, security, the approval of others. As long as you have a personal stake in the world, you are not one with God.

In the East the process of becoming enlightened is made easier, if only slightly, because everyone is raised to know that God is One, the totality of existence. So putting him in a box has no meaning. The fact that God was reflected in hundreds of individual gods to be worshipped doesn't contradict the notion of God as One. Children in India are taught that the image of Krishna or Devi or Shiva, along with the temples devoted to them, are merely a facade, behind which hides Brahman, the true name of God since Brahman denotes everything in creation, plus every possibility that could emerge from the domain of infinite possibilities.

It could be said, with some justice, that a society that knows God is One has failed if it builds so many temples with idols for worship. But I think the case is more complicated. Brahman is also a label, no different from Jesus or the Prophet Muhammad. It's a fairly rudimentary label, since the root word for *Brahman* simply means "to swell or expand."

But Brahman makes the same impossible demand as God does in the West: that you think about everything in existence. The history of religion consists of shuffling God from one box to the next as faiths rise and fall. This was convenient for the world's faiths but disastrous for knowing God. When the Indian seers who wrote the *Upanishads* declared that "the knower of Brahman is Brahman," they understood that God stands apart from anything else we know. The issue isn't how to think about God but how to experience him directly.

This may sound like using mysticism as an escape route for true believers who don't want to be contradicted by reason. "I can't talk about it" isn't a statement you can refute, much less "No one can talk about it." The mystery of God is treated that way all too often. But other things in life can be understood only if you experience them, from the scent of a rose to the taste of chocolate, to the luxurious touch of cut velvet, to music. These sensations have no reality for someone who hasn't experienced them. Music strengthens the case even further, because music changes people. Studies have shown that playing music to Alzheimer's patients seems to reduce their symptoms in a way that no drug can, and although drugs can affect depression, music therapy is promising there, too, as it is in certain cases of autism.

Music bypasses the part of the cortex responsible for rational thought, but naming the location where the brain processes music doesn't tell us why it is therapeutic. Single tones can have a balancing effect, it appears, in some psychological and physical conditions. The stress response can be lessened with soothing music. Some of these findings match common sense—listening to soothing background music settles the jitters of flying for some travelers, and it is so ubiquitous in department stores (presumably to put shoppers in a mood to buy) that we block it out. My point here is that many experiences can alter us simply through our having the experience. God would be the ultimate example.

Besides being futile, some religious thinking causes harm. With seeming inevitability, different faiths, because they disagree, lead to us-versus-them thinking, and then it's a short step to persecution. In our own mental box, "we" are good, devoted, beloved by God, forgiven of sin, and headed for a divine reward after death; "they" are misguided, set apart from God, ignorant, wicked, threatening, and headed for divine punishment after death.

A gruesome fact of religious history in the West is that the first heretics to be burned at the stake were thirteen Catholic clergy in Orléans, France, on December 28, 1022. It is speculated that burning was chosen because of a stricture against the priesthood shedding blood. The charge of heresy was undoubtedly trumped up; the hapless victims were pawns in a political struggle for the throne of France. But as a trigger for violence, us-versus-them was off to a roaring start and only increased as deep divisions grew between Christianity and Islam (igniting the Crusades to save the Holy Land from infidels), the pope versus secular kings, the Eastern Church in Constantinople versus the Western Church in Rome, and even priests versus laypeople, which gave the Inquisition the right to judge the private faith of everyday citizens.

The ultimate us-versus-them thinking separates "me" from "God." Once this separation arises, it brings with it all the problems of duality. It's astonishing that people were ever persuaded to love a God who is set apart from them—usually we fear and distrust "the other." But religion has built in a large dose of fear along with love, as anyone who has ever heard of mortal sin, hell, and damnation knows. I mention these well-worn facts because they lead to a surprising conclusion. If separation from God leads to fear, persecution, and evils done in the name of God, then the only escape is to heal separation. Only a God who is inseparable from us can be real.

What if God *is* reality? Only then would we be free from illusion. If you reduce God to a mental construct, you are stepping into illusion and its many aspects.

God as Illusion

When is God not real?

When he seems to come and go.
When he judges and disapproves.
When he makes demands.
When he is fickle and changing.
When he seems to have abandoned you.
When he answers some prayers but not others.
When there are two contending Gods at war.

I apply the same standards to God that we ordinarily apply to reality. Reality doesn't come and go. It doesn't abandon us. What changes is how we relate to it. Moods rise and fall; pessimism gives way to optimism. Whenever you say "I'm having a bad day," you're talking about a relationship. I know that *reality* is an abstract word, so imagine the air you breathe. The act of breathing is a constant, and Earth's atmosphere is a given. If it weren't for problems like air pollution and global warming, we could leave breathing to the unconscious mind. Yet you can bring the act of breathing to your mind whenever you want. On a beautiful day you fill your lungs deeply, feeling nourished by the air you breathe. Running a marathon, you regulate your breathing to keep the oxygen supply to your muscles constant. Feeling anxious, you gasp in short, ragged breaths.

But to claim that the air has changeable feelings about you, or that it is punishing you one day and rewarding you the next, would be illusory. We are the ones who change; air is constant. The same holds true for God, who has been identified mistakenly as a fickle, changeable, mysteriously unpredictable presence. Such a belief is a symptom of separation; we have to bridge the gap and get closer to what God actually is.

Everyone has an interest in being real. On that basis, we can bypass the debate between believers and nonbelievers. When Lord Krishna tells Arjuna that all roads lead to God, he's making this very point. Reality leads everyone forward. In the interval between birth and death, we all come to grips with reality; therefore, consciously or not, we are coming to grips with God.

But I must pause on a tragic note. Sometimes suffering is so incomprehensible that illusion comes as the only comfort. I say this under the shadow of the horrifying school shooting in Newtown, Connecticut, just before Christmas 2012. A disturbed gunman entered two classrooms with assault weapons, killing six adults and twenty children, almost all six and seven years old. In the wake of mass murder on this scale, pastors come forward, and one said, "This isn't in God's plan." I wondered how many people were comforted by the statement. If there is a moment when a loving God grievously disappoints us, it must be with the senseless death of innocents.

Sometimes you look away and let illusion do what has to be done. God gets off the hook for not saving the children. Insanity makes the killer less than human. Evil gets its day. Gradually the faithful return to their beliefs, while a few more doubters peel away from religion, and the atheists shake their heads over the way people look to God for answers when he is the problem. I didn't want to let illusion take hold, so I wrote a private note to myself: "It's our deepest inner intelligence that mirrors the wisdom of the universe. Ultimately all suffering is the result of the fragmented mind, personal and collective. Violence is rooted in collective psychosis. The cure is transcendence to God consciousness. My challenge is to make this real. In the meantime, each of us must find consolation any way we can."

If God is everywhere, like the air we breathe, why is he so hard to find? Because everything you say about him is open to contradiction. Once you single out any quality, its opposite is just as true. Does God love us and bring good things into our lives? All religions say so. But then what about the bad things? If God causes them too, then he doesn't stand for good. If he can't stop them, then his goodness has severe limitations. So does our own goodness. Why not worship ourselves? (A college student on television commented on why she didn't go to church anymore. "I can't believe in a God who would send me to hell for doing something bad," she said. "If I made my parents mad, they wouldn't throw me in the fireplace.")

No matter how you dice it, every aspect of God winds up biting its own tail.

Protector: If God is here to keep us safe, why are there natural disasters?

Lawgiver: If God hands down the rules of moral conduct, why are we free to be as immoral as we like?

Peacemaker: If God brings inner peace, why does he permit war and violence?

A God who is all things can't be *only* good, loving, peaceable, and just. Whether we like it or not—and mostly we really hate it—we must make room for God's participation in the bad, painful, and chaotic parts of life. Am I saying that God is good and bad, loving and unloving? No. *Any quality you give to God is an illusion.* When in doubt, an easy test is to substitute *reality* for *God*. Is reality loving or unloving? The question makes no sense. Reality is all-inclusive. It simply is. Once your mind begins to wrap itself around an all-inclusive God, one who simply is, you are truly escaping illusion.

Everyone is used to relating. Two people get together, and they either click or they don't. Maybe there is intense infatuation. Love begins to blossom, but at a certain point there are problems. Each person in the relationship has an ego. *I love you, but this is how I do things.* If the relationship is going to survive, "I" and "we" have to come into balance. All kinds of issues must be worked out.

The beauty of relating to God is that none of this applies.

God doesn't have an ego. He always likes what you like. He always wants what you want.

God doesn't have a point of view. He accepts your way of seeing things.

God isn't selfish. He doesn't want anything from you.

God doesn't reject. Whatever you are is fine with him.

If this sounds like an ideal relationship, it is. Human beings have projected their deepest yearnings and feelings onto God, only to be disappointed when their projection didn't yield results. No amount of worship makes God love you better. If God were human, this fact would condemn him to being unloving. In most cases, if you are in a relationship and worship the other person, you will get love in return. The irony is that God, the possessor of infinite love, gets labeled as showing no love at all. The relationship never started in the first place—that was the problem, not a flaw in the deity.

A map for the journey

The key to reaching God is to undergo a shift in awareness. The shift isn't minor or incidental—it's total. Unless we transform our minds, God will remain out of reach. Fortunately, we have a map to guide us. It was drawn collectively by the world's wisdom traditions, incorporating what religion has to say but relying far more on what those who delved deep into their own consciousness have discovered.

Open up the map, and the main features of the path to God are clearly visible. They show us the existence of three worlds.

The Three Worlds

The material world. This is the world of duality. Good and evil, light and dark contend here. Events unfold in a straight line. Each person is a tiny speck in the vastness of nature. We journey through this world driven by desire. God remains out of our reach because he is the one thing that we cannot see, touch, talk about, or conceive of. As long as we remain in duality, the ego-personality dominates. Everything revolves around "I, me, and mine."

The subtle world. This is the transitional world. Good and evil are not rigidly separated; light and dark merge into shades of gray. Behind the mask of materialism, we sense a presence. We move toward it using intuition and insight. Random events begin to reveal hidden patterns. We are driven through the subtle world by a craving for meaning. Nature becomes a stage setting for the soul. Everything revolves around self-awareness and its expansion.

The transcendent world. This is the source of reality itself. At the source, there is oneness, a state of unity. Nothing is divided or in conflict. The veil of materialism has fallen away completely. Good and evil, light and dark have merged. We move through this world guided by our higher being, which is inseparable from God, who is the state of supreme being. The individual ego has expanded to become the cosmic ego. Everything revolves around pure consciousness.

God remains a muddle because these three worlds overlap, undivided by fixed walls. At any moment, you might be living in any one of them or peering across the frontier from one to the next. Awareness takes you where you want to go. Reality remains constant as you travel from one state of awareness to another. But as things stand now, when most of us are attached to the material world, awareness is the last thing we know much about. We are constantly confused about whether other worlds even exist, and when someone steps forward to affirm that they do, they are likely to be greeted with skepticism and hostility.

Faith can go only so far in promising that other worlds exist beyond the one detected by the five senses. Once faith opens up the possibility, we must turn it into a living reality. First we need a clear sense of where we're going. For the sake of bringing order out of disorder, the spiritual map indicates a starting point (the material world), a middle section (the subtle world), and a destination (the transcendent world). It's not really that way, however. Being fluid, awareness can go wherever it likes, whenever it likes.

You venture into the subtle world all the time. Here are some typical experiences in that state of awareness:

You follow a hunch.
You become aware of another person's actual motives or feelings.
You see how you are affecting the people around you.

You feel bonded to another by love.

You stop feeling the need to judge.

You are struck by beauty.

You feel generous of heart.

You want to give and be of service.

You feel inspired and uplifted.

To one degree or another, these are egoless experiences. "I, me, and mine" lose their grip. You expand beyond selfish desires. You intuit that there is more to reality than what your five senses tell you.

You travel into the transcendent world all the time as well, although modern society isn't set up to acknowledge or approve of these excursions. Here are some typical experiences when you touch the highest level of awareness.

You feel light, unburdened, and unbounded.

You see common humanity in every face.

You feel completely safe.

You enjoy being here for its own sake.

A calm stillness appears inside you.

Infinite possibilities seem to open up.

You feel wonder and awe looking out at nature.

You surrender, accept, and forgive.

You are certain that everything matters; things happen
    for a reason.

You feel that perfect freedom is the most natural way to live.

You shift your reality by entering a new state of consciousness. The only boundaries are self-imposed, yet we impose them all the time. We remain stubbornly attached to a core of beliefs that stop our spiritual journey before it has even begun. I can imagine science taking hold with such conviction that the world's wisdom traditions become totally marginalized. No one believes in the subtle world, and the transcendent world is degraded to a delusion.

Yet even on the verge of extinction, spirituality would be revived. Despite all the disappointment in God and the reasonable doubts offered by skeptics—even the unreasonable ones promoted with a whiff of malice by the four horsemen—certain constants remain the same from age to age. They urge everyone to change, and all must be taken into account if you want to know God. These constants are

Desire for a better life

Love

The force of evolution

Experiences of ecstasy and bliss

Curiosity

The growth of wisdom

Dissatisfaction

Dreams

Visions

Inspiration

Personal experiences of God, higher reality, the higher self

These are the drivers of spirituality, with or without religious labels. They came first, before anyone applied words like *God* or *soul*. A decree could abolish those words but not the motivation behind them.

The drivers of spirituality fight against the status quo. They make us into restless creatures who yearn for change. How we respond to them is entirely individual. Indian lore is full of precocious seekers who left home to find God when they were small children. Jesus was wise enough to confound the rabbis at the Temple in Jerusalem at the age of twelve. But as in all things, the extremes are rare because they are so single-minded. At one extreme are seekers who live for personal transformation and nothing else; the world's saints, sages, and spiritual guides need almost no motivation. At the other extreme are the perpetually stuck, people who deny or hate any kind of change; the world's ideologues, fanatics, and psychologically fearful will never be motivated to open up their minds.

The rest of us find our spiritual way more haphazardly. Our path is a crooked one, affected by all kinds of distractions. We are confused and doubting. Inner conflicts cause us to get stuck. But the same forces that create saints are present in your life. What they wait upon is to be noticed. If you are reasonably attentive to what's happening inside yourself, you are already responding to the forces listed above. You envision a better life for yourself. Growing as a person matters to you. You can see the outlines of a better future for yourself.

These everyday motivations are enough. We can reach the most exalted spiritual goal through them. You will hear no mystical voice inside your head, and no hand will reach down from heaven to grab you by the nape of the neck. The whole story is told in a single concept: God is realized in the highest state of awareness. Since everyone is aware, God is reachable by all of us.

Is There a Material World?

've described three worlds, each of which has its own spiritual purpose. The material world doesn't show any physical evidence of God's presence that would convince a skeptic. Atheists often make much of this fact, and their arguments are reasonable, as far as they go. In a violent world, a loving God can't be defended. The existence of lawbreakers makes it unreasonable to say that God has the power to punish wrongdoing. The human rights violations of oppressive governments make an all-powerful God seem like a cruel joke—Stalin and Hitler welded absolute power without the slightest interference from the Almighty. We can concede all these things as they apply to the material world. God becomes real only when you discover that the material world isn't the end of the story.

An Indian spiritual master once told a devotee, "The physical world is very convincing. It seems solid and reliable. How can you possibly escape it? By seeing that this world is actually a product of your mind. Without that realization, the physical world wraps around you like a net. But all nets have holes. Find one and jump through." If you are a materialist, such statements drive you crazy; they seem totally bizarre when the world "out there" is so obviously real. I won't repeat the arguments against accepting the world "out there" as a given. Our concern now is to jump through the net.

Escape is possible by seeing a simple but radical truth: All worlds are created in consciousness, including the physical world. Find a way to free your consciousness, and nothing will ever be the same.

On the subtler levels of reality, God possesses the love, goodness, and power attributed to him. Our challenge is to connect these subtler levels to the material world. If we succeed, the picture changes. On the spiritual path, you discover that being human is multidimensional, and the subtler dimensions contain great power. There will even be enough power to change events "out there" in the material world.

Mind over matter

The New Testament contradicts the rules of physical reality using a famous analogy: "Because you have so little faith. I tell you the truth; if you have faith as small as a mustard seed, you can say to this mountain, 'Move from here to there' and it will move. Nothing will be impossible for you" (Matthew 17:20). Jesus's words have sustained the faithful and aroused skeptical disdain almost equally.

The basic claim he makes is that mind moves matter. In the human body this claim is undeniable. Thoughts and feelings create molecules in the brain that communicate to the rest of the body. If you are intensely afraid, your hormones—in this case, the stress hormones cortisol and adrenaline—send a very different message from the one they send if you are in love. Moreover, to have any thought, image, or sensation, the brain must operate through electrical signals and chemical reactions that bridge the synapses, the gaps between brain cells. These chemicals are in a constant state of flux, being created and destroyed thousands of times per second to keep up with your shifting mental state.

If we move outside the body, the situation seems very different, but Jesus explicitly declares that a mental state—faith—can create a shift in the material world. How? The religious explanation is that God, because he favors the righteous, will intervene to alter physical reality for them. But too many martyred saints have died in agony to trust that the righteous have much pull in this department. What we want instead is a natural explanation, and for that, mind over matter must be reduced to a common denominator. Earlier I nominated consciousness as being common to all experience, inner and outer, listing the elements necessary to make anything real.

Intelligence

Intention

Attention

A bridge from mind to matter

An observer

A connection between events "in here" and events "out there"

Jesus is talking about the last item on the list—for him, the bridge between "in here" and "out there" is faith. God has created mind and matter together, and if you have enough faith, God gives you control over them together. In Jesus's example, something very tiny (a mustard seed) is juxtaposed with something huge (a mountain), but the exaggeration is simply for effect. Faith doesn't have a size, big or small. It's a state of mind; either you are in that state or you aren't. The point is easy to miss, as believers often do. They interpret Jesus as giving faith such unimaginable power that even a tiny bit of it must be nearly impossible to acquire—after all, who among us is moving mountains?

Certainly the four Gospel writers are quite consistent about putting mind over matter. Jesus tells the disciples that they will acquire remarkable powers through faith. "He that believeth in me, the works that I do shall he do also; and greater works than these shall he do" (John 14:12). In the Sermon on the Mount, Jesus degrades the material world, putting the sacred world above it. The sacred world follows different rules. That's the whole point of the examples he chooses: The birds of the air are fed by Providence even though they do not store up grain, and the lilies of the field are beautifully arrayed even though "they neither toil nor spin" (Matthew 6:28).

The rules of the material world point to a different conclusion. Each of us toils in our own way, and in our struggle to build a worthwhile life, we cannot rely on faith alone. Faith doesn't pay the gas bill, much less move mountains. If you are devout enough, you cannot simply ignore this disappointing fact, and if you are a confirmed skeptic, you cannot simply ridicule it. But there is an alternative approach, known as seeking. You can seek to build a living connection between mind and matter, between what happens "in here" and how that affects events "out there." The connection isn't a given. If it were, prayers would reach God automatically, like telephone calls. The seeker wants to find out why God responds to us some of the time—as countless believers attest over the centuries—while ignoring us even in dire need most of the time.

I'd suggest that the spiritual purpose of the material world is seeking. Mind meets matter every day. Which is more powerful? The Book of John's declaration "In the beginning was the Word, and the Word was with God, and the Word was God" (John 1:1) is a stark statement about mind coming first and the material world second. For the Gospel writer, creation itself was an act of mind, the thinking or utterance of a word. As a seeker, you try to get back to the creative source in yourself, not as a word but as a state of mind filled with untold possibilities. There's nowhere else to go if you want to solve the mind-over-matter problem.

Wisdom traditions agree that the source of creation is inside us. In one of the great texts of Vedanta, the sage Vasishtha declares, "Dear ones, we have created each other in our fancy." This claim, preposterous at first sight, becomes inescapable if God *is* reality. Then the logic is simple and ironclad, a logic that sustains every spiritual tradition, East and West.

If God is the creative source of everything,
And if God is in us,
The creative source of everything is in us.

A seeker is searching for God, reality, and the true self all at once. To do that, one must escape the net that traps us in the physical world. We must redefine ourselves as multidimensional. Seeking begins in the physical world, however, because we are all entangled in it from birth. It's a tricky business to be in the world but not of it. Physicality is incredibly convincing. Is there really a way to jump out of the net?

When you have a dream, you are in the dream world—running around, flying, seeing animals, people, and stranger creatures perhaps. But as soon as you wake up, you realize that you are not of that world—that it's not the reality you come from. To the enlightened, the same holds true of the events we experience when we're awake, going to work, raising a family, and so on. We are in that world, but it's possible to wake up and realize that we are not of it. To the Vedic seers, the material world is as much a dream as the dreams we have when we're asleep in bed. In a famous verse, Vasishtha contemplates a spiritual version of what modern physics calls the multiverse, where countless universes exist in their own dimensions:

> In the infinite consciousness, universes come and go like par-
> ticles of dust in a beam of sunlight that shines through a hole
> in the roof.

This is a spiritual version of the multiverse, as becomes clear in another verse: "Whatever the mind thinks of, that alone it sees." All roads lead to God only if all roads lead to consciousness first.

Dawkins and company don't concede the existence of any level of reality beyond the material world. It's easy to sympathize with their position, even if they state it with such open hostility. Seeking, as an inward project, is unknown to them, as it is to many people. Religious history is a centuries-old record of seekers going in different directions, encountering every possible pitfall along the way. So if we are to do better, we need to be very clear about where our search is going.

What is seeking?

Seeking isn't a fixed activity with a single goal—it has shifted over time. In the medieval era, seekers wanted to get a reward in heaven, and although we cannot know if they found it, every aspect of social life, from wandering friars to great cathedrals, was focused on it. The vast majority of people who were alive in the Middle Ages, a huge span of eight hundred years (from 400 to 1200 CE), had no hope of acquiring power or money. They could love one another, but they lived in a "vale of tears" where everyday existence was a struggle to survive. The best they could hope for was to find refuge in monasteries and convents. Large masses of people took that path. But in a way, by seeking refuge from a cruel world, they turned their backs on faith. To judge by the results, *The Age of Faith,* as a rubric for the centuries dominated by Christianity, is a misnomer. If Jesus is telling the truth, faith is what makes it possible to create an ideal world where every desire is fulfilled: "Ask and it will be given to you; seek and you will find; knock and the door will be opened to you" (Matthew 7:7). If you seek, the sign of success is that desires come true. You have proven that mind is the ultimate power. Whatever a Christian was meant to do to turn this promise into reality—have faith, align with God's will, or be without sin—nothing was enough for the wretched mass of medieval believers.

When the world was a harsher place, seeking led directly to renouncing the world. Because we have easier lives today, we have much less reason to renounce the world, but a lingering belief that the world is a vale of tears makes many people feel that religion is opposed to fulfilling one's desires. If there are approved Christian teachings in favor of desire, few believers know about them. In fact, modern believers are not versed in religious teachings much at all—a 2012 Pew Research poll posed thirty-two basic questions about religion, and the people who got the most right were the atheists, with an average of 20.9. (Peter Gomes, who preached to a liberal congregation at Harvard College, asked a group of them what the epistles in the New Testament were. A shy hand went up: "Are they the wives of the apostles?")

Today, seeking has become almost entirely private; there is no consensus about the goal. It takes courage to step away from the religion you were brought up in. The Protestant theologian Paul Tillich wrote a best seller in 1952, *The Courage to Be,* which is steeped in the angst of the atomic age. The Holocaust and the terrors of two world wars had scraped belief in God down to the last few chips of paint. There was a widespread acceptance that life must be meaningless. Tillich saw the situation and asked, "Why are we here in the first place?" Life, he said, poses that question automatically. If being alive makes you ask why you are here, you automatically want to find an answer. The two activities—asking the most basic existential questions and answering them—form a circle. Questions lead to answers, for no other reason than that you are alive.

I don't think society has gotten much beyond the situation Tillich describes. God has been worn down to a nub, and terrorism is an everyday threat, even as the threat of mass nuclear destruction has begun to wane. The seeker doesn't have a platform of belief to stand upon. Finding the courage to be means finding the heart to go beyond meaningless existence.

This isn't pretend or make-believe courage. In many ways seeking is harder than having faith. Having faith is passive; it doesn't demand constant self-examination the way seeking does. Believers are nervous that if they lose their faith, they will be left with aching doubt and uncertainty. So they must fend off doubt. Seeking, on the other hand, begins with doubt as a foundation for finding out the truth. It welcomes uncertainty as better than inflexible, dogmatic certainty. Seekers are courageous enough to be different, to renounce the comfort of a community inside church walls. They are open to considering spiritual ideas from other traditions beside Judeo-Christianity. For all these reasons, a modern secular society, far from being the enemy of spirituality, offers fertile ground for it.

Whenever someone tells me that they have found God, I'm tempted to ask what he looked like. If they gave me a definite answer, I'd have to tell them to keep looking. This is what Buddhists mean when they declare, "If you meet the Buddha on the path, kill him." A preconception never works—it will only lead you to run into the thing you've already imagined. God—or the Buddha—will remain unimaginable. But I don't say this to seekers, because it sounds defeatist. I just point out that the issues surrounding God are secondary. You have to know reality before you can know God.

If I had to name one motivator that turns someone into a seeker, it would be this: People want to be real. The will to believe, which in earlier centuries was focused on God, has morphed into a yearning for a real life, one that holds together, that is rich in meaning and purpose, that brings fulfillment. The Holocaust and every other mass horror created a terrible sense of unreality. Feeling unmoored has become so pervasive that we rattle along working frenetically and getting distracted even more frenetically, unaware that any other reality exists.

But at the beginning, when modern life first became frightening in its unreality, only a few witnesses were brave enough to face it. Primo Levi was an Italian Jew who was transported to Auschwitz and survived. In the late 1940s, just a few years after the Russian army captured the camp and freed the prisoners, Levi wrote movingly about how it felt to come back home to his native Turin, where everyone wanted to forget the Nazis and return to normal joys and desires. At first Levi found himself talking incessantly about Auschwitz—he stopped strangers on the street and passengers on trains, unable to keep silent. This did him some good; at least he was reconnecting to other people. But he no longer felt real, the way they seemed to feel. He felt set apart, isolated, a wandering ghost. His struggle to feel real again sometimes went to extremes. A friend recounted a disturbing incident when Levi came across a wild persimmon bush and attacked it maniacally, clawing at it and chewing on the fruit.

Although trained as a chemist, Levi felt driven to put his Auschwitz experience into words. The result was a classic survivor's memoir, *If This Is a Man.* "Probably, if I had not written my book," he told his biographer, "I'd have remained one of the damned of the earth." Levi took the courage to be to an anguished extreme. But I'm grateful that he— and others who have struggled to return from severe depression, heartbreaking trauma, and even madness—has shown us that being real can be such a powerful drive. Translated into normal life, seeking has some crucial ingredients that bind all of us together.

What Makes a Seeker?

The desire to be real
The courage to step into the unknown
A refusal to be fooled by illusions
The need to feel fulfilled
The ability to go beyond material satisfactions
An intimation of other levels of existence

You are a seeker if these ingredients exist inside you. They may only be seeds; nonetheless you feel a stirring within you, some sort of desire percolating inside. For religious people, the word *desire* can be worrisome. Doesn't God want us to renounce desire? If, as we are told, sex, money, and power are pitfalls on the way to heaven, the enticement of desire is contrary to God. Yet Freud called sex, power, and the love of women the primary goods in life. (He was speaking to a male world.) Human nature was designed to pursue these things. If that's true—and millions of people live their lives as if it is—how can seeking offer something better?

In this regard, seekers present a misleading public face. On the one hand, the project becomes something religious, a kind of hunt for the unicorn, except that the mythical beast is God. On the other hand, New Age spirituality has become synonymous with crystals, angels, channeling spirits, and communicating with the dead. It's easy to mock such things; they get thrown onto the pile of evidence that atheists have amassed about the irrationality of religion. The deeper issue is our yearning for reality and what is to be done with it.

Making it work

Now it's time to get real. The material world is chaotic, filled with events beyond anyone's personal control. To be a seeker, you are required not to conquer the chaos but to see through it. The Vedic tradition uses a clever metaphor for this: A seeker walks through a herd of sleeping elephants without waking them up. The elephants are your old conditioning, which insists that you are weak, isolated, and abandoned. You can't fight this conditioning, because once you wake it up, your fear, insecurity, and certainty that you must struggle to survive will have tremendous power. Once the elephants wake up, they'll trample you.

So the world's wisdom traditions figured out another way. Sneak past these obstacles, without trying to fight them head on. Shift your allegiance, silently and inwardly. Stop being ruled by the chaos and start being ruled by your core self. Let me map out what the process entails.

In practical terms, the process follows this precept: "Strip away your illusions, and what is left must be real." The material world rests upon illusion, as quantum physics has proved. Yet the mythology of materialism persists. How does it affect you personally? Consider the rules that govern material life, such as struggle, self-defense, competition, class divisions, and the attempt to control nature. The assumptions that underlie these rules are hard to challenge. They are rigid and, for most people, a given. Let me spell out a few, as they pertain to various levels of our existence.

Scientific level: The rigid assumption here is that human beings are small specks in the vast, cold cosmos. All uses come down to matter and energy, including the mind itself, which is a by-product of how molecules behave in the brain. The laws of nature are fixed and immutable. Whatever happens inside the mind has no effect on reality "out there," which is devoid of consciousness.

Social level: The main assumption here, which drives endless consumerism, is that acquiring material things leads to happiness. More is better. Money is the most valuable commodity in life. You solve problems by climbing the ladder of success and wealth.

Spiritual level: The main assumption here is that spirituality is a matter of hard work, like everything else. You climb the ladder to God by striving. You get demoted when you become lax. Every faith sets down dogmatic rules for arriving at success. Those who obey the rules earn their way to heaven. This whole scheme has rightly been dubbed spiritual materialism. That is, the soul is put to work just as the body is in the material world.

These aren't passive influences. They have trapped us into the danger that Vasishtha warned against: The mind sees only what it has created. The inability to discover inner power can be traced directly to the "mind-forged manacles" that William Blake lamented. Although I'm arguing that materialism isn't reality, I'm not saying that a deliberate lie is at work. Arch-materialists, including Dawkins and company, are describing what they see. Their fatal error is to miss that the mind makes every version of reality, using its invisible creative power.

To become a seeker, you don't have to walk away and exist as an outsider from society; you aren't required to turn your back on those who love you or to proselytize a set of new beliefs. Those are the customary trappings of religious conversion. Because religion has monopolized that field, it seems wise to take a completely different tack. I'd suggest a simple version of "the courage to be." Reexamine your present situation. Sit down with a sheet of paper and confront what your existence is about.

Here's a simple format. In one column list the external things you put effort into, for example:

Family
Friends
Career
School, higher education
Status
Wealth
Property and possessions
Politics
Hobbies
Exercise
Going to the movies
Sex
Internet and social media
Video games
Television
Travel
Church attendance
Service organizations
Charity

Beside each category, put down a number. It could be the number of hours a week you devote to this activity; it could be how much you value the activity, on a scale from one to ten.

In another column, make a list of the inner activities that you put effort into, such as

Meditation
Contemplation
Prayer
Self-reflection
Stress management
Reading spiritual material, including poems and inspirational
     literature
Psychotherapy
Personal growth
Intimacy
Bonding with someone else empathically, or out of compassion
Appreciation and gratitude, toward yourself and others
Exploring the world's wisdom traditions
Taking a period of silence
Going on a spiritual retreat

Rate these things, too, with a number, reflecting the value you put on each one or how much time you devote to it.

When you have finished, compare the two lists. They will give you a rough sense of where your allegiance lies between the inner and outer. I'm not suggesting you play a spiritual blame game—almost everyone predominantly pursues outward activities. The material world holds us fast. It's quite all right for inward activities to take place in the material world; they can be part of one daily routine. (Jesus pointed to the need for peaceful coexistence when he spoke of rendering unto Caesar what is Caesar's and unto God what is God's.)

Unless you devote time and attention to inward things, you are not seeking. Being pious and doing good works are not a substitute. They remain all too often on the external plane. For someone who needs a set of spiritual goals, I'd begin with two that have nothing to do with religion and everything to do with getting real: find your center, and then run your life from there. Both goals are necessary. If you leave out one, the other will have limited use.

Finding your center means settling into a stable, coherent state of awareness. Outer forces do not dominate you. You're not restless, anxious, worried, or unfocused. You are finding your center whenever you

Act with integrity

Speak your truth

Remain unswayed by the need to be liked

Stop people-pleasing and placating

Do not fear authority

Protect your personal dignity and respect the dignity
    of others

Don't keep secrets from yourself and those closest to you

Honor confidences

Remain self-reliant, not dependent on others

Do not blind yourself with denial and self-deceptions

Refuse to turn against others for ideological reasons

Practice tolerance

Become slow to anger and quick to forgive

Aim to understand others as you understand yourself

The second goal, running your life from your center, means obeying subtle inner guidance, such as instinct, intuition, love, self-knowledge, trust, and compassion. It also helps to know what *not* to do. You aren't living from your center whenever you

Focus on external rewards (e.g., money, status, possessions)

Crave approval from others

Go along to get along

Endorse social conformity

Open yourself too easily to outside influences

Uphold rigid moral guidelines

Put too much emphasis on rules

Set yourself up as an authority

Compete as if winning is the only thing that matters

Demonize your rivals and competitors

Gossip and belittle others

Hold on to prejudice or ideology

Seek revenge

Skirt the truth

Practice us-versus-them thinking

Keep your inner world a secret

Once you achieve the two goals, your material world will hold together in the same way that you hold together. Inner and outer will no longer be two separate domains; you've made them connect. You can operate from a core of integrity and express your true self. That's how a person learns to overcome the material world's chaos and fragmentation.

This project of seeking that I've outlined is existential, to put it in a word. The courage to be has traced a path, not to the God of faith but to a solid sense of what it means to be real.

When you begin to suspect that you are the author of your own
existence, seeking has begun.
When you start to use your awareness to actively shape your life,
seeking has brought an answer.

When you look around and know that reality is based entirely on consciousness, seeking has reached its goal.

The next stage is to journey deeper, always moving toward the source of creation, which is where the real power lies. Seeking takes place in the material world, but finding happens somewhere else.

The Subtle World

I f you go into any bookstore—some of them are still around—and throw a rock, it has a good chance of hitting a book about science and religion. The vast majority of these books call for a truce between two camps that have traditionally struggled against each other. In July 2005, science had no choice but to shake hands with its old nemesis: The prestigious journal *Science* celebrated its 125th anniversary by citing 125 open questions that science had yet to answer. The top two were these:

What is the universe made of?
What is the biological basis of consciousness?

After so many years of tremendous scientific achievement, it's shocking that no one even has come close to answering these questions—in fact, the latest investigations only deepen the riddle. As we saw, just 0.01 percent of the cosmos is filled with atoms forming all the visible stars and galaxies. Roughly 4 percent of the cosmos gathers in the remaining invisible atoms, as interstellar dust and free-floating hydrogen and helium atoms. The remaining 96 percent of "stuff" appears to be nonatomic, and it disobeys basic rules about gravity and the speed of light. So it isn't stuff at all, not by any measure of the visible world. To say that physics explains space and time is like saying that someone with 4 percent eyesight sees the whole landscape.

As for the biology of consciousness, no one has shown that consciousness even has a biology. Brain imaging, although a huge advance in looking beneath the skull, reveals where blood is flowing. That isn't remotely the same as showing how a chemical soup—a mélange of water, blood sugar, DNA, and potassium and sodium ions—learned to think. It is just as likely that a thinking universe decided to create the brain.

If you can't answer the preceding questions, which are like the ABC of reality, your theory of where human beings came from is, to say the least, questionable. As a scientist, you have no choice but to keep insisting that the answer will be found one day, probably soon. (This was *Science*'s position. The editors based their list on a survey of one hundred leading scientists, asking them to focus on questions that might be answered within twenty-five years.) It's rather late in the day to ask for more time when what you are after isn't a grand goal (like the long-awaited Theory of Everything) but only a credible starting point. God is all about starting points. A matchup between spirituality and science is inevitable. Both of them peer into a level of reality across the border from the visible world. Both confront the wonder of nature and the strangest of all phenomena, as Einstein saw it: that nature can be understood in the first place.

I'm calling the invisible domain the subtle world. We've arrived there by the path of faith. Science gets there by using a chain of steps that peel away reality like an onion or a Russian doll, with smaller and smaller matryoshkas nested inside each other. But the subtle world isn't exclusive territory for either side. If it's real, it's real. Science may disdain the path of faith, but that only shows its disdain for the very consciousness that links all mental activity, whether it is prayer or bombarding protons to release Higgs particles.

The onion layers as peeled back by science are straightforward propositions that all scientists agree upon:

Is life reducible to biology? Yes.
Is biology reducible to chemistry? Yes.
Is chemistry reducible to physics? Yes.

Is physics reducible to mathematics? Yes.

Is mathematics an activity in consciousness? Yes.

In public forums and private conversations, I've presented a number of prominent scientists with this sequence, and they show no hesitation all the way to the end (only a slight suspicion, perhaps, about walking into a possible trap). The squirming begins when I say, "It looks like life is reducible to consciousness, right? We've used your own methods to get there." Generally they meet this conclusion with a shrug of the shoulders. One neurologist conceded that this was the hardest chain of questions he had ever confronted. A cosmologist accused me of reductionism. But I hadn't laid a trap. Consciousness pops up as the basis of creation, whether you start from God or from the test tube. In one case, matter disappears into mind; in the other case, mind emerges as matter. The subtle world is their common denominator.

Faith is supported by logic, but it's hard to convince someone if your logic isn't theirs. Dawkins has alienated even those who share his atheism because he arrogantly supposes that he took out the patent on rationality. No logic works but his. Even so, until very recently, forcing science and religion into a shotgun wedding satisfied no one. Dawkins and company reflect a social rift as much as anything else—if you "do science," you aren't likely to keep professional company with those who "do religion." The two courses of study don't overlap at university; the two kinds of work don't share the same building.

Yet the tools for making God real are the ones that construct the real world. They can be stated in a small handful of principles. No one needs to take out a patent on them. If they pertain to reality itself, they should be acceptable to both believers and skeptics.

Principle 1—You are not a passive receiver taking in a fixed, given reality. You are processing your experience at every second.

Principle 2—The reality you perceive comes from the experience you are processing.

Principle 3—The more self-aware you are, the more power you will have as a reality-maker.

None of these principles will come as a surprise. *Consciousness* and *creator* have been important words in my argument all along, but you must test each principle; you have no other way to reclaim your role as a creator. If you don't test them, you have passively accepted the skeptics' position, which maintains that consciousness is totally unreliable because it is subjective. "I like lollipops" can't be equated with "The sky is blue." One is a fickle personal experience; the other is a scientific fact. But as we've seen, the distinction is baseless. It takes consciousness to make the sky blue. It takes consciousness to think in the first place. Skeptics warn us not to trust the events that happen "only in your mind," when the truth is that the entire world happens only in your mind.

Invisible signals

The real question is "How far can you trust?" Can you trust your mind when it takes you across the border from the visible world? That's the crux of it. Consider what it means to surrender to God. This has always been portrayed as an act of faith, which means—if we are brutally frank—that most reasonable people will reject it out of hand. Surrendering means trusting in an invisible force beyond the five senses. Obviously you wouldn't let God drive your car. No invisible force is going to cook dinner tonight. The material world works according to its own rules. If you stop there, surrender isn't really necessary—you can trust the material world in an everyday way. No one has ever surrendered to God except by mistrusting the material world and following hints that lead in another direction. These hints are like peeks behind the smoke and mirrors of a magic act. They show you how the tricks are done.

Since the subtle world touches all of us, hints about it cross your path every day. Reflect on how many of the following things have happened to you. The list is long, but it's important to realize that you are already connected to a deeper level of consciousness, if only through momentary glimpses.

Hints from the Subtle World

Connecting to deeper consciousness

You have an "aha" or "eureka" moment.

You feel a burst of heightened reality, as if things suddenly became clear to you.

You are struck by awe and wonder.

You are visited by a sudden sense of pervasive peace and calm.

Inspiration comes to you. You have a leap of creativity.

Events seem to form a pattern, and suddenly you see what the pattern is.

Unexpectedly, you feel loved, not by a specific person but simply loved.

You think of a person's name, and the next minute that person telephones you.

A random word comes to mind, and you then run across it in your reading or conversation immediately afterward.

You foresee an event, and it comes true.

You have a particular desire, and it gets fulfilled as if on its own.

You run into meaningful coincidences, when two events coincide and mesh.

For a whole day, things seem to organize themselves, falling into place without effort.

You feel the presence of someone who has passed away.

You see another person's aura, either as visible light or as a subtle
   sensation of light.
You detect charisma, a strong personal force, from someone else.
You feel that someone else radiates pure love or a holy presence.
You sense that you are guided.
You are certain that your life has a purpose, which may feel
   predestined or beyond what your ego wants.

It takes only a speck of self-awareness to notice such hints. They
present flashes of mystery. *Something* is asking to be noticed. Now ask
yourself a key question. How many of these hints did you trust? Did
they make a difference in your outlook or your everyday response to
life? The amount of trust people place in them varies enormously. One
"eureka" moment can change an entire life, but that is rare. What is far
more common is to receive a hint about the subtle world, only to let it
pass as you return to living the way you normally do.

The arena of subtle perception is fragile at first. This is the main
reason doubt arises about the power of consciousness. We take awareness for granted, and when events jump out of their usual groove, we
don't know how to respond. A friend told me about visiting an Indian
holy man—in this case, a woman, actually, born in poor circumstances
who grew up to be surrounded by devotees. My friend was quite reluctant to go. "I was asked by a follower of the holy woman, and I've always
been embarrassed to tell him that his beliefs lowered him in my eyes.
The notion of surrendering to someone else appalled me. Why on earth
would a person give up their freedom that way?"

My friend arrived to find the holy woman sitting in a large tent; it
was crammed with people and redolent of sandalwood incense. She sat
on a low dais, a small figure dressed in a sari, to all appearances indis-
tinguishable from anyone else.

My friend had a surprising reaction. "I expected to shut down, seeing hundreds of people focused on this unknown person, most of them

bowing down as they approached her. She smiled at each and gave them a light embrace. It was a strange sight, the very picture of what I disliked about the whole guru science, but for some reason I felt quite relaxed and comfortable."

Shy to approach the holy woman, my friend sat in the back of the tent. But she had heard about *darshan,* the traditional Indian practice of receiving a blessing in the presence of a holy person. An impulse told her to go forward and receive *darshan,* so she gradually made her way toward the front.

"I have no explanation for what happened," she later told me. "People were jostling me on either side, but I kept inching ahead. As I did, my mind became quiet. The crowd didn't make me feel agitated or impatient. A little closer, and this inner quiet became very peaceful. Closer still, and I sensed a sweetness inside, the way you'd feel around a happy infant—only this sweetness went deeper.

"Finally I was next in line. The holy woman smiled at me and lightly put her arms around me. She uttered a few words in my ear that I didn't understand—later I was told that this was her blessing.

"What if I had been given a photograph of that moment? It would show a tall white Western woman stooping over to be hugged by a little brown Eastern woman. Yet the experience was indescribable. I felt an intensity in her presence that only the word 'holy' can describe. At the same time, it was like meeting myself. The little brown woman wasn't even there. She was—what?—the symbol, the carrier, the messenger of a divine encounter."

A powerful hint indeed. Afterward my friend found herself puzzled and deeply touched at the same time. She's still working out what happened. I'm using the word *hint* because plunging directly into the subtle world would be so overwhelming that our minds shut out the possibility. We permit ourselves only hints and glimpses. The world would be a strange place if every other person were blinded by the light, like Saul on the road to Damascus. We've conditioned ourselves to see through a glass darkly. When his traumatic conversion turned Saul into Paul, he used the metaphor of seeing through a glass darkly because his perception had changed forever. The subtle world became his home, compared to which the normal world was a place of dingy shadows.

The hints won't stop coming unless you persistently block them out, which some people do. The subtle world awaits the moment when these scattered signals begin to matter. Then a shift occurs. Your consciousness starts to free itself up. A dramatic example of this would be the long-term response of people who have had near-death experiences. Most report that they no longer fear death and dying, while some go further and report a loss of anxiety altogether. You and I don't go around feeling a constant fear of death, because it is embedded in the psyche at a subtle level. This is also the level where release comes. Whether one believes in near-death experiences or not, release of fear takes place, which indicates that the subtle world has been contacted, and the contact led to a practical result.

Once the subtle world starts to matter to you, it will allow you to overcome more than hidden anxiety. It is the realm of light, where *light* means "clear perception, a state of transparency." Consciousness is meant to be free. You have only to provide an opportunity and encourage every step of expanded awareness. How is that done?

You remain open-minded.
You don't listen to the voice of fear.
You don't allow yourself to escape into denial.
You take a holistic point of view.
You question the narrow boundaries of ego.
You identify with your highest impulses.
You are optimistic about the future.
You search for the hidden meaning in everyday events.

These are what I call *subtle actions*. You don't take them on the material level. The hints left by the subtle world require a subtle response.

Subtle action

All of us are used to subtle action, although we don't use that name for it. All subtle actions are choices. Imagine that you have left on a vacation, and on the way to the airport a nagging thought comes to you: *Did I lock the front door?* perhaps, or *Did I leave the oven on?* At that moment, you are confronting yourself, and a choice arises. Do you return home and double-check, or do you trust that nothing is wrong? The first is action in the material world, while the second is subtle action. You may not see a difference, but consider this. In the material world, we worry, double-check, fret, and so on out of a sense of insecurity. But intuition, which is subtle, doesn't fret or worry. When you decide to trust your feelings, you are making your choice on the subtle level. (Simply stating the difference doesn't mean that you can ignore every worry. You need to follow a process before trust becomes real.)

Subtle actions pervade life. If you trust that your partner loves you, that's a subtle action. A less secure person asks for reassurance, such as ending every phone call with "Love you" in order to hear "Love you, too" in return. Only words and deeds can assuage their insecurity, but they can't trust their own inner world. Inner trust and mistrust can affect the course of a lifetime. A child who has been well loved by his parents will almost always go through life feeling secure about his lovability. At the subtle level, lovability is a settled matter. But if a child grows up doubting that she is lovable, she will experience nagging doubt at the subtle level. What happens then? She will spend years trying to calm a sense of restlessness, dissatisfaction, and insecurity, and a fear of never being good enough.

The basic needs that religious people direct to God are also subtle. *Lord, make me feel worthy. Lord, make me feel loved. Lord, make me feel blessed.* If you direct these appeals outward, you cannot trust that God will reply. You're like a telegraph operator at an isolated station tapping out a message with no security that the lines aren't broken. Only after you experience the state known as "God within" do you trust the connection. God is disconnected in the material world but has a presence in the subtle world. This isn't the end of the journey, but through subtle action, followed by a real response, the divine starts to matter. To lose fear or to feel blessed isn't a mystical response. You think and behave differently from someone who hasn't undergone a subtle change.

An Indian parable comes to mind as an illustration. Once there was a monk traveling by himself and teaching the dharma, the right way to live spiritually. As he made his way through the forest, he came upon a large clearing and sat down to rest.

Just as he opened his sack to take out some food, a thief happened to pass by. He saw that the sack contained an enormous diamond. When the monk finished his meal and set out on his way again, the thief ran ahead and hid in the bushes. Soon the monk approached, and the thief leaped out. The monk calmly asked him what he wanted.

"The diamond in your bag," the thief replied.

"You followed me all this way just for that?" the monk asked. He took the diamond from his bag and held it out. "All right, take it," he said.

The thief greedily snatched the diamond and hurried away. He hadn't gone far when he looked back to make sure the monk wasn't coming after him. What he saw stunned him. The monk was sitting cross-legged under the stars, meditating peacefully with a look of complete bliss on his face.

The thief went running back to him. "Please," he begged, "take your diamond back. I only want to learn how you could lose it with so much peace."

The story is about the difference between human nature that hasn't been transformed and human nature that has. Subtle actions matter deeply; they provide direction to our whole existence. At every moment of the day we are arriving at hidden crossroads and making choices that lead one way or the other.

To trust or mistrust
To surrender or control
To let be or interfere
To pay attention or ignore
To love or fear
To engage or escape

We can distinguish subtle actions that have positive results from those that don't. But they shouldn't be taken as directions in an instruction manual. There is no approved set of choices that are always right while the others are always wrong. Love is the greatest good in life, but sometimes you have reason to fear. Not interfering is often wise counsel, but sometimes you must intervene. The secret to making the right choice is to be comfortable in the subtle world. When it is your home, you see clearly the right choice to make. The situation speaks to you. The gap between the question and the answer gets ever smaller. When these things start to be familiar, you have learned to trust your instincts and operate through intuition.

Instinct and intuition are genuine skills. Most of us merely make stabs in the dark because we have spent so little time developing these skills. Our inner world is confused and conflicted. Great artists are beautiful examples of skilled intuition. Imagine standing next to Rembrandt as he paints. His palette contains the same jumble of colors as that of any other painters of the day. The subject before him is perhaps a rich Amsterdam lady wrapped in a stiff white lace collar and gold jewelry. (Rembrandt's subjects were often eager to wear their wealth on their backs.) Rembrandt's hand dabs at his paints, then at his easel. These are the ordinary actions of any professional portrait painter.

Yet after a few sittings, a transformation has taken place. Instead of a portrait, a living human being has emerged on canvas. With his subtle skill, Rembrandt has intuited what this lady's character is. She displays a hidden range of qualities (vanity, melancholy, sweetness, naïveté) that shine through the pigments. These inner qualities can't be translated into mechanical technique. They require a direct connection between the subtle world and the painter's hand, which is why we stand in awe-struck admiration and say, "He has captured her soul."

Not just geniuses but anyone can develop subtle skills. New mothers do it all the time when they learn to read the signals given off by an infant. (In tribal Africa, mothers carry their naked babies around on their backs. The mother knows immediately when to take her baby and hold it out to urinate or move its bowels. There is an instinctive bond, and no accidents.) The issue isn't whether you have subtle skills—I'm sure you have many. But experiencing God isn't a single skill. God is everywhere in the subtle world. The divine doesn't appear by glimpses, in peak moments with sudden blinding light. The divine is constant; it is we who come and go.

Until the subtle world becomes your home, you can't help but come and go. Repetition and practice are part of the learning curve. The trick is to know that you are in the subtle world to begin with. The level of the solution is deeper than the level of the problem. Staying at the level of the problem therefore leads to frustration.

You've probably met people who are constantly aiming for self-improvement, who say things like "I'm learning to be less angry," "I'm learning how to trust more," or "I'm learning how to be less controlling." Somehow this learning never ends. Despite all their struggles, they are stuck with anger, mistrust, and control issues. (People who take anger management courses, for example, sometimes wind up angrier afterward. Likewise, the benefits of grief counseling are suspect and highly unpredictable.) Why does this happen? There is no cut-and-dried answer, but a range of possibilities comes into play.

> The person didn't reach the subtle level but struggled at the level of ego, self-doubt, and blame.
> They lost heart when they met with inner resistance.
> They lost motivation after one too many setbacks.
> Their approach was confused and filled with contradictions.
> They didn't take real responsibility for their behavior.
> They were lacking in self-awareness.

To put it simply, most people approach the subtle world haphazardly, rather like "cheasters," casual Christians who attend church only at Christmas and Easter. Our failure to find God can be traced back to our habit of coming and going rather than making a home in the subtle world. Just so, our failure to play the piano well can be traced back to the moment we dropped piano lessons; our failure to perfect your golf swing, or to be creative, resulted from lack of practice. As banal as it sounds, finding God depends on regular practice.

I'm not here to catalog the failures of seekers who never find what they are searching for. It's far more important to arrive at a trustworthy path to the goal. The subtle world may lie in the unknown, but it is always open.

Leading your brain

The most trustworthy path is to take a mind-body approach. In any state of awareness, the brain processes experience; a mundane experience like walking the dog is on the same plane as an exalted experience like hearing angels sing. The brain must be adapted to process both. As a child, you went through very specialized adaptations in your brain to learn how to read. Your eyes had to be guided to focus on small black specks on a piece of paper; they had to move in linear fashion from left to right and then down to the next line. Your cortex had to decode the black specks into letters. Your memory committed itself to building up a vast library of words and ideas. Becoming literate was like moving to a new world.

Your shift away from materialism will be far more radical, because you give up all attachment to the physical universe as your fixed reference point. An impulse of love will gain more power than a thunderstorm. The sight of a rose in your mind's eye will have the same status as a rose held in your hand; both are products of consciousness. Just as it adapted when you learned to read, your brain can adapt to experiencing God. When you commit to a strategy of shaping how your brain processes perceptions, your spiritual vision will become practical. In fact, this serves as the litmus test—if your brain hasn't been retrained, you will not discover anything real in your spiritual search. You will still be in the net, waiting to find a hole to jump through.

The brain cannot reshape itself; it functions as a mechanism for processing what the mind wants, fears, believes, and dreams about. By becoming more conscious, you automatically begin to lead your brain where you want it to go. In the Age of Faith, every person was conditioned to process daily life in terms of God. There were sermons in the stones; a fallen tree was a telegram from the Almighty. Today the opposite is true. The stones are dumb; a fallen tree is a random event. The human brain has learned to adapt to *any* reality. That's a great gift, because it means you can lead your brain into the subtle world, which becomes real as your brain adjusts to a new landscape.

Your brain, despite its marvels, requires basic training when you learn any new skill, and finding God is a skill. New neural pathways must be formed, which will happen automatically once you put focus, attention, and intention behind it.

Below are seven strategies for processing the subtle world, one for each day of the week. Each day focuses on a different exercise to make you feel comfortable with your inner world. Be easy with each exercise, repeat them over a period of time, and you will witness a genuine and lasting change in your consciousness.

Day 1

Be Generous of Spirit

Old pathway: Holding on to what is yours
New pathway: Sharing yourself

Exercise: Today be aware of old habits that cause you to react with "me first." Watch yourself holding back instead of giving. If you see hints of selfishness, greed, fear of lack, fear of loss, and other kinds of contraction around giving, stop and take a deep breath. Cut off the reaction, and go back on the self. Wait and see if a new way of responding comes up. It's okay if it doesn't. Just stopping the old reaction is a step forward.

To lay down a new pathway, look for one opportunity today where you can be kind, affectionate, or appreciative to someone. Anticipate someone's need before they ask. See what you can do to go out of your way to help. Ask what it means to be generous, and see yourself in that role. Act on your generous impulses instead of shrinking away from them.

Day 2

Be Loving and Lovable

Old pathway: Suppressing love
New pathway: Expressing love

Exercise: Today your goal is to turn repression into expression. Inside us all there are feelings and impulses that we resist. We don't express them even when they are completely positive. It may be healthy or socially prudent not to express how hostile you feel at a given moment, but repressing something as positive and basic as love is self-destructive. Happiness consists of knowing what you need and gaining fulfillment from someone who wants to meet your need.

Since giving is easier than receiving for most people, show some aspect of love today that you would normally repress. This doesn't mean that you suddenly come out of your shell and say "I love you"—although that is often a very welcome thing to say and to hear. Instead, think of your mother or someone else who loved you in a very natural way. What did she do to express love? She looked after your needs, she put you ahead of herself, she didn't judge or criticize, she helped heal your wounds, and she supported you when you were nervous, afraid, or insecure. Find a way today to enact that role for someone else.

It is impossible to turn "I am not lovable enough" into "I am perfectly lovable" overnight. A process is involved. What made you feel unlovable was a series of messages from other people; these negative messages became incorporated into your self-image. So let's reverse the process. If others give you positive messages that you are lovable, your self-image will shift in that direction. Bit by bit, you will earn a new self-image.

Be aware of yourself today in terms of love. Watch to see if you push away other people's positive messages. See if you fall into the groove of acting neutral, indifferent, or careless with others. If so, stop. All retraining requires that you stop doing what doesn't work. If you simply stop, that is a step forward. But also add to the new pathway. Be someone who is worthy of love. A smile, a kind word, any act of bonding—these small daily things tell other people that you care. Most love isn't romantic. It's an expression of a warm heart, and the one thing that every warm-hearted person does is care. Instead of worrying if you will ever find the right one to love you, be the right one. The more you express love, the more your higher brain will automatically react in loving ways.

Day 3

Let Go

Old pathway: Holding on to resistance
New pathway: Surrendering to what is

Exercise: Today you need to let go of something. Keep your attention on this, and when a moment arises when your inner voice says "I'm right, dammit," or "I'm not giving in," just stop. You don't have to do the opposite of anything. Merely pause and be self-aware. Notice that you are clinging, holding on, demanding that the situation change. How does this make you feel? Almost always, holding on feels tight, constricted, angry, and stressful. If you feel any of this, walk away and relax. Do deep breathing or meditation. Center yourself before you react.

Letting go is both emotional and physical. You are opening a pathway of acceptance. Whatever your inner voice says, reality is simply what is. You need to look at "what is," which means dropping "what should be." Don't think of this as surrender in the sense of losing. Think of it as being more open, letting your brain gain more information. At a higher level, you are also calling upon the brain to deliver better responses that suit the situation.

Being self-aware will alert you to your negative reactions. In the past, the old pathways gave you two options when you felt negative: shut down or act out. Most people shut down, since they've learned from painful experience that acting out their judgment, anger, resentment, and ego gets poor responses from others. Yet this was never an either/or situation. Instead of shutting down or acting out, you can simply be aware. When you do that, you let in the light of consciousness. Your higher self is actually nothing more than expanded consciousness. By holding on to anything, you squeeze it into a narrow place in your mind—the mental equivalent of folding your arms tight across your chest. You can spend a lot of time with tight-folded arms, a clenched jaw, and beady eyes, or you can notice what you are doing and stop.

The mental equivalent works the same way. You can cast other people as wrong for a long time, or you can notice what you are doing and stop. The process of letting go begins here. In this case, once you stop clenching inside, your brain is automatically freed up. Over time openness becomes a habit. The new pathways replace the old by gaining fresh experiences. Once you actually look for proof that holding on isn't working, it's easy to find. What takes patience is to find the rewards in letting go. Life is hugely complicated; shutting yourself up into a small room delivers a safer reality. But once you let life flow in by no longer resisting, letting go becomes easier, and then you see that life is yours to experience as an individual. Bliss is universal; finding our own kind of bliss is a privilege that belongs only to you.

Day 4

Find Your Fulfillment

Old pathway: Routine
New pathway: Satisfaction

Exercise: Today you need to break out of predictable routine. That's easy to do—too easy, if all we're talking about is asking for poached eggs instead of scrambled, or turning the channel from *Sunday Night Football*. Routine is rooted in the brain. It's a form of survival when in truth it never ran a risk of not surviving. Most people's lives are established when it comes to the basics of food, shelter, and clothing. The fact that we can take survival for granted, however, doesn't convince the lower brain. It is constantly trying to shore itself up against famine, aggression, exposure to the elements, and a dangerous environment. Hence the sense of risk, amounting to dread, when people are cut off from their familiar routines.

Your goal today is to learn to expand beyond your brain's habit of equating *new, fresh,* and *unexpected* with *alien, threatening,* and *anxious.* Be aware of how you structure your whole day around making yourself feel safe. Protecting yourself is a lower-brain instinct. But remember, the lower brain never evolves; it continues to do what it did millions of years ago. Only your higher brain can evolve, but it won't if you live behind mental barriers. Break out of the security systems you've built around yourself, even for a little while. When you do, what happens? You will walk around feeling insecure, and that's your actual reality. We are not talking about foolish risk-taking. We are talking about the root of insecurity, which is the belief that the universe would never uphold our existence.

To dispel that deep sense of insecurity, you must go through a process of retraining your brain. Give it room to evolve. The lower brain won't go away; you need its protective instincts some of the time, although very rarely. Most people are protecting themselves from imagined threats. But if your higher brain dominates, the protective voice will grow smaller and less anxious.

Imagine that you have been dropped unwillingly into the middle of Haiti after its devastating earthquake or into Malaysia after its tsunami. You will probably go into some kind of anxiety or panic. Now imagine that you have voluntarily gone to those disaster sites to help. You are there for a higher purpose, something deeply meaningful to you, and therefore, the voice of threat is rendered marginal.

Meaning overrides insecurity. That's the key. So today find something to do that expresses your purpose. Let life support your purpose. Be decisive; know what you are about. If you cannot think of anything that fits the bill, then read a book about someone in real life who inspires you, a potential role model. Absorb yourself in the path that this person took. Now sit back and consider whether you have been given a clue about your path. Clues are always present. It's part of the dharma, the cosmic force that will uphold anything you intend for a deep level inside yourself.

Day 5

Enable Your Healing

Old pathway: Passive neglect
New pathway: Active well-being

Exercise: Today your goal is to help your body's healing system. Healing system is a relatively new term medically, in that in brings together several of the body's systems. The immune system may be central to healing a wound or infection, but emotional healing involves the brain, exercise involves the muscles and cardiovascular system, diet involves the digestive system, and so on. People pop vitamin pills thinking that they are helping to fend off disease, but the benefit is minimal and mostly unnecessary given a healthy balanced diet. When the same person refuses to address damaging stress in their lives or long-held anger and resentment, the result isn't passive; the healing system is meeting a serious obstacle.

Today, break through your passive neglect. When you brush your teeth, think about the whole issue of your dental health. When you eat breakfast, consider how to nurture your body. When you take the elevator instead of the stairs, consider how good it is to be active. As you do these things, check in on how you feel. The reason you neglect yourself always has an underlying feeling attached to it.

You are tuned to the world, including the subtle world, through body awareness as much as mental awareness. Are you happy to tune in to yourself physically? Many women, indoctrinated to have a poor body image, don't want to tune in at all. They use worry and self-judgment instead. They accuse their bodies for not being perfect, a form of rejection that carries a hidden price: They are rejecting the body's healing system at the same time. Thus it becomes an annoyance when the body signals discomfort, and if the discomfort is actual pain, their only response is anxiety and panic.

You can avert all this by tuning in, not out of anxiety, but as your body's ally. In turn, your body will become your ally. The most positive signal you can send every day is to be aligned with balance in all things. Your body is constantly in the state of dynamic equilibrium called homeostasis. This is the same as a car idling at the stoplight or setting a thermostat and walking away. Homeostasis is meant to be disturbed, to be thrown off its set point. The reason is that a body at rest also needs to move at a moment's notice. If you decide to run after a cab, rush to the phone, or enter a marathon, homeostasis gives you the flexibility to do so.

Passive neglect reinforces the body at rest; it chooses inertia over dynamism. What helps homeostasis to remain dynamic, flexible, and available at the touch of intention? All kinds of things, as long as they are the opposite of inertia. Exercise wards off physical inertia. Taking an interest in life wards off mental inertia. Best of all, self-awareness enables the whole mind-body system to be dynamic, because self-awareness makes room for spontaneity. The best kind of freedom is unexpected, because it renders you open to surprise, passion, and the unknown. So see if you can trigger those things in your daily life. Surprise yourself; take an interest; find something to be passionate about. These are all deep forms of healing, and when you pursue them, you are truly finding your healing.

Day 6

Raise Your Expectations

Old pathway: Limited expectations
New pathway: Unlimited potential

Exercise: Today you need to be fulfilled, not by waiting for a magical day in the future but by changing the pathways of fulfillment. Fulfillment is multidimensional. It feels satisfying physically, emotionally, and spiritually. The ingredients are, first, a general sense of relaxation and contentment in the body, along with the absence of tension and discomfort. Second, at the emotional level, you feel a sense of personal satisfaction; you are living your life well. With this comes an absence of threat, isolation, loneliness, and emotional baggage. Finally, on the spiritual level, you feel at peace and centered, connected with your highest self. This comes with an absence of doubt, of fear of death, and of abandonment by God.

Although only a sketch, this picture of your multidimensionality shows you where to look for fulfillment. Any of these dimensions will do, and if you truly pursue physical, mental, and spiritual satisfaction, they will merge. All the pathways will be open to the many avenues that fulfillment comes from. There is no set recipe. It's true that giving brings fulfillment to many people, and others experience satisfaction only when being of service. These are general conclusions only. Because you are multidimensional, any map you draw leads to where you want to go.

The chief obstacle is limited expectations. Whether they admit it or not, most people are unfulfilled because they set their sights too low. They have in fact achieved what they imagined would make them happy. For decades psychologists looked at what makes people miserable and psychologically impaired. In the new field of positive psychology, researchers instead look at what makes people happy, but their findings are full of contradictions.

Everyone tries to be happy; everyone pursues the thing they think will make them happy. But it turns out that human beings are bad predictors. When we get the thing that should make us happy, it doesn't. New mothers, for example, often feel frustrated and depressed by taking care of their babies; some mothers rank caring for small children as a source of unhappiness, along with doing household chores. Having money makes people happy only up to a certain point. They reach a nice level of comfort, but then extra money increases their unhappiness by adding responsibility and worry. And once you have enough money, you receive diminishing returns from getting more. The second Porsche doesn't carry the thrill of the first; the tenth time you stay at the Ritz, the glamour has mostly rubbed off.

Wealth aside, the essential reality is that achieving fulfillment requires having higher expectations. As you go through your day, experiencing all kinds of things, pause and ask yourself, "Honestly, what is this doing for me?" The answer won't be cut and dried. Some things will be more fulfilling than you might suppose; others will fall flat. Then ask yourself, "What would be more fulfilling instead?" In other words, embark on a journey of discovery. You will quickly find that discovery isn't a piece of cake; obstacles and limitations will lie in your way.

Be aware of the following kinds of limitations: Thinking that you don't deserve better. Fear of not being accepted. Fear of failure. Fear of sticking out too much from the crowd. Anxiety over leaving your old ways behind. For many people, happiness equates with settling. They choose good enough because it's safe. But good enough means that your dreams will be so limited that fulfilling them will bring only small satisfactions. Take a second look at the people you associate with. Their expectations are likely to be your own, because in all likelihood you want to fit in with your own crowd. You aren't asked to disapprove of your friends or yourself—quite the opposite.

Choose the person you most admire among your circle, or the one whose dreams secretly match yours. Here is a living example of how to expand your expectations. You can get closer to this person, ask for advice, and share your heart's desires. Yes, this means taking a risk. Exposing who you want to be isn't necessarily safe. But finding out who you want to be is crucial, because it will keep your eye on the prize. You will accept constant growth, an unending journey, expanding horizons. Achieving fulfillment isn't like building a wall brick by brick until you stand back to admire the finished product. It's like stepping into a river in which you can't step into the same place twice.

The one image is static; the other, dynamic. The one is fixed securely in place; the other leads who knows where. You have neural pathways to deal with both extremes. Stability is important, but so is dynamism. Most people are so imprinted to be secure that they don't have much play on the dynamic side. Their landscape features more walls than rivers. As you go through your day, try to be aware of how your personal landscape looks. That's the first step in getting around the walls. Some will need tearing down; others will need climbing over or sneaking around while not knocking them down. It feels good to live with as few walls as possible if they are the kind that shut out new possibilities. See if you can take one deep breath of real satisfaction today. In that lies the path to lasting fulfillment.

Day 7

Let It Be

Old pathway: Struggling to achieve
New pathway: Using least effort

Exercise: Today is about learning to let it be. The basics are simple: Intend for a certain outcome, let your intention go, and wait for the result. There is nothing esoteric about these steps. You go through them every time you send an order to your brain, such as wanting to raise your arm. The intention is carried out automatically. You don't stand watch to see if your brain will respond the way you ask it to. The feedback loop between intention and result runs smoothly and automatically.

The art of being consists in bringing the same trust and effortlessness to other aspects of your life. The difference is that in the West, people keep events "in here" apart from events "out there." Claiming that one's intention can affect an external situation sounds normal in Eastern spiritual traditions, which hold consciousness to be everywhere, both "in here" and "out there." One worldview is dualistic; the other is unified. But terminology is irrelevant; the proof is in the pudding. Can you have an intention and allow it to manifest without struggling to achieve your goal?

The world's wisdom traditions say that you can. "Letting it be" means being connected to the same source in pure Being as everything in the cosmos. When this connection is strong, having a desire "in here" leads to a result "out there" automatically, because the underlying unity transcends boundaries and artificial separation. To arrive at the point where you are completely connected is a process, one that takes place through the brain. As in the previous exercises, you only need to become more self-aware.

In practice, what I'm asking you to do is this: Have one intention today, let go of it, and see what happens. If you get the result you want, appreciate the fact that you connected, you tuned in to the mechanism of least effort. "Least effort" is the same as letting your Being do the work. If you don't get the result you want, shrug it off and try again with a new intention. Many times, however, the result won't be obvious. You will come close or sense that things worked out approximately as you wished.

This is part of the process, so notice that you came close, and accept the result you received. (Most of the time you will have to do more work to achieve what you wanted, but that's okay.) In this exercise, there is no failure. Creating a strong connection to your Being is the same as creating any new pathway. You are making progress if any of the following indicators appear:

It takes less effort to get to a result.
You feel less stressed about getting a good outcome.
People begin to cooperate with you more easily.
You sense that everything is going to be all right.
You start to have strokes of luck.
Events mesh together in synchronous fashion.
Results start to appear more quickly.
Creative solutions appear as if out of nowhere.

None of this is mysticism. Every life already contains synchronous happenings, strokes of luck, and happy coincidences. Instead of accepting that these are accidental or random events, you can now look upon them as a sign that making a connection is very real and possible. Mastering the art of being takes time and self-awareness. But your brain is designed to forge the ultimate pathway to fulfillment, which is effortless.

Let's say that you have begun the process of reshaping new pathways. At first this requires effort and patience. You must address the old pathways, which represent imprinted memories, habits, and conditioning, over and over. You are changing the default mode of your brain, and it takes conscious attention to do that. But the project is highly rewarding, and if you persist, various signs of progress will appear, including the following:

Your internal dialogue quiets down.
Negative responses diminish.
You resist and control impulses more easily.
A sense of meaning grows.
You begin to feel cared for.
You feel less regret over the past and less anxiety about the future.
Decision making becomes clearer.

At a certain stage, you reach a tipping point. Having done the work of imprinting your brain to have new responses, you can trust those responses. This opens the door for Being. You can "let it be" when your brain starts taking care of you. You already trust your brain to take care of you in countless ways. It automatically controls hormone levels, respiration, the sleep cycle, heart rate, appetite, sexual response, the immune system, and much more. So the art of being isn't foreign to you; it is second nature.

Transcendence: God Appears

We have reached the point where a complete transformation is possible. A God who hardly matters can turn into a God who matters more than anything else. This kind of transformation leads to freedom. Who wouldn't want to accept Rumi's enticing invitation when he says,

> *Out beyond ideas of wrong-doing*
> *and right-doing there is a field.*
> *I'll meet you there.*

> *When the soul lies down in that grass*
> *the world is too full to talk about.*

There's the prize. But at the same time, transformation is threatening. Our core beliefs define us. We resist having them ripped away from us just as we fear radical surgery.

To see God without illusions, we've had to overturn conventional religion. We had no choice. Religion does its worst because of lower-brain responses (fear of punishment, us versus them, the need for security and safety) mixed in with tribalism, cultural mythology, childhood fantasies, and projections. The whole mélange was unhealthy. More to the point, it wasn't God. Dawkins and company were absolutely right to attack these illusions. But they didn't lay a hand on God, because they never dismantled their own bundle of illusions.

What does that take? During the dark days of the Civil War, Abraham Lincoln realized that the Union would defeat the Confederacy, but the old United States couldn't be reassembled without a drastic change. Slavery had not been prohibited in the Constitution. Lincoln had grown up with the same mentality of racism as almost everyone else. The inferiority of black people was an ingrained belief. As with all core beliefs, its strong emotional hold was hard to shake.

In Steven Spielberg's moving film *Lincoln,* there's a finely imagined scene where Lincoln's mind finds an escape from racial prejudice. He is sitting alone in the war room, which is deserted except for his two young secretaries. The mood is somber, naturally; moments of quiet only brought home the true horror of the bloody conflict. At such a moment, what does Lincoln bring up? Euclid, the great Greek mathematician. A dropout after grade school, Lincoln had educated himself by becoming a voracious reader, and in the theorems of Euclid, he discovered a logical proposition: *If two things are equal to a third thing, they are equal to each other.* He repeats this basic piece of logic in a fervent voice, but Lincoln doesn't reveal its hidden significance. We are asked to grasp the implication ourselves, something like the following:

If a white man was created by God,
And if a black man was created by God,
Black and white men are equal before God.

The higher brain, we might say, proved its superiority. Trained to value reason, the cortex couldn't retreat into lower responses to the slavery issue (self-protection, suspicion, hatred, fear), even though these responses still existed, even in a great man like Lincoln. His ultimate view of the slavery issue was spiritual. His personal journey was a struggle—to the end, Lincoln never had a close friend who was black—but logic aided him to get there.

There's something explosive in simple logic. It has the power to make the mind question everything it has hitherto taken for granted. The things we take for granted are more powerful than anything else. They support our worldview, holding it together, secure and safe. In this book, true knowledge of God was unreachable as long as we took for granted three things: reality, consciousness, and God himself. God was simply there in the background, doing nothing. Being conscious was the opposite of being asleep; it had no hidden power. Reality was the material universe and the stuff that filled it.

We've now exploded all of those assumptions and have arrived at a simple piece of logic that can free the mind totally, once and for all:

> If God is reality,
> And if reality is consciousness,
> Then God is consciousness.

The trick is to make this logic livable. It remains dead as just a set of ideas. The mistake when we try to think about God—pro, con, or in between—is that God is not an idea. I was testing out this book on social media (it seemed appropriate to keep up with the times), and one day I tweeted, "Militant atheists and religious fundamentalists are both obsessed with God. But what obsesses them is an idea. God is not an idea. God is consciousness." A heated discussion arose, and one person tweeted back, "You're in the same boat with Dawkins. Consciousness is just your idea of God." But that's not so. God is reality itself. He isn't a thing, which is what fills the material world. He's not an image, feeling, sensation, or thought, which fills the subtle world. God inhabits a third world beyond anything that words and ideas can describe. This is the transcendent world, the place where true knowledge of God is found.

The mystery of Oneness

You get to the transcendent world by first arriving at a dead end. Thinking must hit a wall. This is bound to happen for one inescapable reason. Our minds are designed to process opposites: light versus dark, good versus evil, inside versus outside, subjective versus objective. Duality is the name of the game. God, however, cannot be described from the state of duality. He isn't here or there; he's everywhere. He doesn't know this or that; he knows everything. To borrow a metaphor from the Vedic tradition, looking for God is like a thirsty fish looking for a drink of water. What you seek is all around you, but you don't realize it. A fish might leap up and find a place that is not ocean. We can't jump out of the everyday world to find a place that is not dual. God, it must be admitted, is everywhere and nowhere at the same time.

It would seem that finding God is self-defeating, since our minds are set up to experience only duality. One approach might be to empty your mind of all opposites. Since God has no opposite, what you will be left with is Oneness. The way it works is something like this. A crisis has arisen, and people are rushing around in a panic. The crisis could be anything—a hurricane, a bank failure, a political upheaval. You are tempted to join in the rush, but you tell yourself, "God isn't found here. He isn't the crisis or the solution but both. He isn't action or inaction but beyond both. He isn't panic or calm but beyond both." By examining every detail of duality, you stop being attached to mental constructs and the emotions they arouse.

Still, it would be hard to imagine anything less suited to everyday life. Constant rejection isn't practical, not when you have to choose between A and B. Do I want oatmeal this morning or toast and coffee? Neither one is God, yet I have to eat breakfast. Choices are inescapable. They are the essence of life as long as we remain in duality. So what good is Oneness when it comes to leading your life? What can it actually *do*?

Human beings have pondered this question and wound up in a bad state. Religion began with the right answer. Going back to its roots in India, religion was grounded on the certainty that God creates, governs, and controls the universe. Therefore God is the source of all love, beauty, and truth. God's perfection can never be shattered. Divine light radiates through every speck and particle of the world. Yet this certainty, instead of making people feel optimistic and cared for, did the opposite. They felt unworthy and punished. The gap between perfection and imperfection never went away. People gazed at God across an unbridgeable gap and despaired.

Eventually the strain between a perfect God and an imperfect world led to a crack in the cosmic egg, which we call science. Oneness was dismantled into measurable facts. Psychology shifted. Ordinary people resented that a perfect God lorded it over them. Online Richard Dawkins reposts for his followers his reasons for being an atheist. Some examples:

I'm an atheist because I choose knowledge over mythology.

I'm an atheist because I don't want to be associated with the heinous teachings and actions of a so-called peaceful religion.

I'm an atheist because after I rejected organized religion, "spirituality" had nothing left to hold it up.

These are like the hostile emotions of a prisoner who has escaped his jailer. They persist even now, four hundred years after Galileo and Copernicus broke the Church's monopoly on truth. Medieval Christians' anxiety at being sinners has morphed into outrage today. But worried or angry, the problem of duality remains. Thomas Aquinas wasn't wrong when he said that all causes need a source that isn't caused. He wasn't wrong to say that a world filled with design needs a source that didn't have a designer, or that the creator had to be uncreated. Science is making the same point when it says that time and space must have a source that is beyond time and space. God talk has turned into physics talk; the dilemma remains the same.

Bridging the gap between duality and Oneness seems like a classic case of "you can't get there from here." Yet there is a way forward, derived from wisdom traditions that look at Oneness not as an unreachable God but as our source here and now. Listen to the South Indian spiritual master Nisargadatta Maharaj as he advises a worried questioner:

> Q: I am never sure of what reality is.
> A: As long as you allow yourself an abundance of moments of
> peace, you will find reality.
> Q: I did try.
> A: Never steadily. Otherwise, you would not be asking such
> questions. You are asking because you are not sure of yourself.
> And you are not sure of yourself because you never paid
> attention to yourself, only to your experiences.

The tone is bracing—Maharaj isn't going to let the questioner off the hook—but the way forward is clearly laid out as Maharaj expands upon his answer.

> Be interested in yourself beyond all experience, be with
> yourself, love yourself; the ultimate security is found only in
> self-knowledge.

This is the same answer given by Vedanta, the oldest and most honored spiritual tradition in India. *Reality is located in the self.* To understand why this is the right answer, we must define *self* differently from the "I" that thinks, feels, and moves through the world. That self constantly creates doubts and questions. The self that is certain about reality has a wider vision. It looks at its own awareness, leaving aside daily experiences, to discover the source of reality.

Maharaj goes on to tell the questioner how vital it is to shift his attention in the direction of self-awareness:

> Be honest with yourself and you will not feel betrayed. Virtues and powers are mere tokens for children to play with. They are useful in the world but do not take you out of it. To go beyond, you need alert immobility, quiet attention.

God is reached by "going beyond," which is the definition of transcending. There is no other way to get past the dead end where thinking stops being useful. Quiet awareness must step in. If it wants to, awareness is capable of going beyond the material and even the subtle world.

Dawkins and company dismiss the whole project of "going beyond" as pure delusion. The self is the last thing they trust. I've had several head-to-head exchanges over this with Michael Shermer, the editor of *Skeptic* magazine, who is as stubborn in his materialistic viewpoint as anyone but not hostile or demeaning. I might pose the question, "Who are you?"

Shermer replies, "I am the sum of the processes in my brain."

I point out that he said "my" brain. "Who is this 'me'? Don't you want to know?"

"No," Shermer replies. "The self is an illusion. There are only brain processes."

"If that's true," I say, "you're telling me that you feel okay about being a zombie."

Shermer shrugs and smiles. "You use language to confuse people. I never ask myself such questions when you're not around."

Shermer is enamored of Dennett's zombie metaphor for the deterministic brain, as are many movement atheists. Besides, no one really believes that his own self is an illusion. We innately trust what we think; we accept our own point of view. If we didn't, it would be like asking a stranger where the nearest gas station is, and he replies, "Two blocks away. But I'm a liar."

Ninety-nine percent of scientists have no need to ask "Why am I?" They have experiments to run and data to collect. Even so, science has hit the same dead end that forces thinking to give up. The Big Bang is as inconceivable as God. We can't envision it, since it was invisible and silent and neither hot nor cold. (All these qualities require the five senses, which didn't exist.) Time and space emerged from the Big Bang, so we can't ask "where" or "when" it occurred; both concepts depend on time and space already being here. In short, science confronts the pre-created state with no trustworthy way to cross the gap.

Fortunately, a dead end for some is an open door for others. You don't have to stare at God while remaining stuck in an imperfect world. Quite the opposite—Oneness can solve the woes of everyday life. In the *Gita,* Lord Krishna declares that all suffering is born of duality. If so, then a step out of duality is a step of healing. God becomes useful once the transcendent world is reachable.

Bridging the gap

You cross the gap all the time without knowing it. You make sound out of silence and light out of darkness. Nothing you perceive around you—not this page, not this room, not this house—has any reality except through you. How do you do it? By crossing the gap. The transcendent world isn't a faraway place you might get to someday. It's the workshop of creation where you go to find the raw material of reality. A painter reaches for his paints to make a picture. Your raw material is nothing more than a possibility. A possibility occurs in the mind;

through the act of creation reality emerges. Now we see why there have to be three worlds:

> The transcendent world is a field of infinite possibilities. It is the starting point, the womb of creation.
> The subtle world brings a possibility to mind as an image. Something real is taking shape.
> The material world presents the result. A new thing or event is manifested.

All three worlds are in fact real, not just the end point, where the result appears. Depending on your state of consciousness, depending on which world you inhabit, reality is completely different. The Vedic tradition provides a clear map of the people who inhabit each world.

When you are free, silent, at peace, and completely self-aware, you inhabit the transcendent world. Labels applied to such people are *Buddha, Christ, mahatma, swami, yogi, the enlightened, the awakened.*

When you are creative, imaginative, intuitive, insightful, and inspired, you inhabit the subtle world. Labels applied to such people are *visionary, dreamer, genius, sage, seer, shaman, artist,* and *psychic.*

When you are involved with physical objects and sensations, you inhabit the material world. The blanket label for this is *normal.*

You can see that human beings live in multiple dimensions. The rules change from one to the other. If a bus hits you in a dream, which is a department of the subtle world, your body isn't injured. In the material world, it is. But getting hit by a bus doesn't prove that the material world is the only reality. Each reality forms a stable framework of its own. If a piano string breaks, you can't play that note, no matter how inspired you are. But the note still exists in your mind, because the subtle world precedes the material world. Without music, no one would build a piano in the first place.

We're not going to wade into the boggy marsh of metaphysics. The issue is practical: When you cross the gap and come back again, what is actually happening? A possibility comes true. Look at three such possibilities, each arriving at a different result:

You want a name for an Australian animal that hops across the landscape with its young in its pouch. From the world of all possible words, you find *kangaroo*.

You want to see the creature that matches this word. From the world of all possible images, you fetch the picture of a mother kangaroo balancing on her tail while a joey peeks out of her pouch.

You want a real kangaroo to touch. From the world of all possible objects, you fetch a live kangaroo.

No one has any trouble with the first two examples, but they balk at the third. Surely fetching a word or an image can't be the same as fetching a live kangaroo. But I can show you that they are the same. What is a live kangaroo made of? The look of it, the feel of it, the smell of it; its weight and solidity; its shape and the way it behaves—all of these qualities, when fitted together in the right way, create a kangaroo, and since each is created in your awareness, so is the animal itself.

I realize that I might be creating a queasy feeling inside, since we accept that "of course" kangaroos exist without us. Actually, there's no proof of that and never has been. It's just part of the psychology of certainty to posit a fixed world with kangaroos hopping around in it. We must shift into the psychology of creativity. A creator is constantly making possibilities come true. All that it takes is to be comfortable in all three worlds of the creative process:

Transcendent world: You are comfortable here when you can experience all possibilities. Your awareness is open. You are connected to the source. Your consciousness is merged with the mind of God.

Subtle world: You are comfortable here when you can hold on to your vision. You trust yourself to follow where the mind goes. You aren't bound up in resistance, objections, skepticism, and rigid beliefs. Inspiration occurs as a normal part of your existence.

Material world: You are comfortable with your personal reality. You take responsibility for it. You read the world as a reflection of who you are and what is happening "in here." As the reflection shifts and changes, you track the changes occurring inside yourself.

Qualia and the creator

Put all this together, and you have the special relationship that exists between human beings and God. It's a creative relationship. It straddles the gap between the uncreated and the created. I hope this special relationship no longer sounds strange.

I've tried to use ordinary words to ease you into realms that most people consider mystical and therefore far away. The only technical term I want to introduce is *qualia,* because it will make you a more confident creator. At its most basic, *qualia* is the Latin word for "quality," meaning the sight, sound, touch, taste, and smell of things. Expand the meaning one step, and *qualia* also applies to mental events. The redness of a rose in a florist shop is a qualia, but so is that same redness in the mind's eye. The brain center for seeing a rose "out there" or "in here," which is the visual cortex, processes them the same way.

It's easy to get stuck on the paleness of a mental image compared with a real rose. No one bleeds from the thorns of a mental rose. But vividness and paleness aren't the issue. The same process creates a rose "in here" and "out there." Besides, dreams can be so intense that you wake up disappointed—the real world feels flat by comparison. For artists, the discrepancy can be very wide, leading John Keats to write, "Heard melodies are sweet, but those unheard are sweeter."

What makes reality personal is the unique way you mix and match qualia. No two people do this in exactly the same way. Take a common experience: You are walking down the street, and a big black dog suddenly runs in your direction. For person A this isn't the same experience as for person B. Here are two possibilities. Person A was once bitten by a dog, remembers the pain of being bitten, avoids dogs, hears the black dog's bark as threatening, and sees its open mouth as a weapon of attack. Person B is the dog's owner, loves it, feels relieved that her missing dog has returned, hears its bark as a greeting, and sees its open mouth as a smile. Two different realities, each depending on the qualia that are made to fit like pieces of a jigsaw puzzle.

You don't observe yourself assembling your experiences, because creation happens instantaneously. To see the pieces of the puzzle, we've taken a snapshot, stopping the flow of time, dissecting an organized picture into small ingredients. If you expand qualia fully, everything becomes an ingredient, including feelings, sensations, memories, and associations. Each experience gets assembled out of qualia. The picture doesn't assemble itself. It only seems to.

To become a creator, the role you were born to fill, you must take control over your experience. You choose which qualia to plug in. If you are afraid of dogs, your past experience has accumulated to support your fear; new input can replace those impressions. To treat that phobia, you can gradually reshape the brain's ingrained reaction. If you see a big black dog coming at you, there's no time to create a new reaction. But on your own you can desensitize your fear by taking gradual steps: looking at pictures of lovable dogs, visiting a pet store, touching a friendly dog that's held on a leash. Even more powerful is to gain direct control over your mental response. Fear is fixed and frozen. You can loosen it up and make it malleable instead. Imagine a frightening dog, then make it larger or smaller in your mind's eye, run it backward or in slow motion: This kind of mental "Photoshopping" puts you in control, a necessary step when fear is controlling you.

Fear is an inner event, but what about the dog itself? Surely you didn't produce a Doberman pinscher out of nowhere. But nowhere is exactly where it came from. A dog is created out of molecules and atoms, which in turn are created out of subatomic particles that wink in and out of the quantum field. "Out" means that they go into the pre-created state. They return to their source, which is beyond time, space, matter, and energy. Here nothing exists except possibilities. (To use a technical term, a subatomic particle that has disappeared from the material world is in a "virtual" state.)

The cycle that carries everything from uncreated to created occurs constantly; it is the basic rhythm of nature. The brain also processes reality through a cycle that turns off and on thousands of times per second. The key is the synapse, the gap between two neural connections. A chemical reaction jumps the gap (this is the on switch), and then the synapse is cleared for the next signal (the off switch). There are other basic on-off switches, keyed to the positive and negative charges of ions passing through the cell membranes of neurons, but the template remains the same. To a neuroscientist, the brain's ability to process reality looks incredibly complex. How do millions of separate signals get orchestrated from all parts of the brain to deliver a single picture of

the world? No one knows, even remotely, because when you examine
the brain, you are looking at a piano played by an invisible pianist—
somehow eighty-eight keys move together to create music. Only in this
case, a quadrillion synaptic connections flash on and off (a quadrillion
being the estimated number in an adult brain).

Watching them doesn't tell us how sight, sound, taste, texture, and
smell are created. Whatever is happening in the gap between creation
and the source of creation goes on under the table. We can't see it, only
the physical result. Even less can we see how two brain cells, each with
identical DNA, emitting the same chemical and electrical signals, manage to produce sound in one part of the brain and sight in another.

Unless you are blinded by your allegiance to materialism, it's obvious that brain cells can't see or hear in the first place. This fact is supported by the simplest test: if you peer inside, the brain is dark and
silent. *Something* creates glowing sunsets and the clap of thunder, along
with all the ravishing sights and sounds of the world. That something is
personal; it's creating your world right this second. Genesis is now, but
it isn't happening in the brain.

The creator behind the scenes is consciousness. It is using the brain,
just as a pianist uses a piano. Whatever consciousness wants comes into
existence. Whatever consciousness blocks doesn't come into existence.
The choosing happens out of sight, but never out of mind. Why do you
have eyes? Because the mind wanted to see, and it created eyes for that
purpose, just as it created ears, nose, taste buds, and the whole mechanics of perception.

"No, this cannot be," a skeptic will object. Evolution created the
human eye over billions of years, starting with the impulse of one-celled
organisms to seek the light. This objection doesn't hold water. It's like
saying that piano keys evolved before music was invented. The piano
is an instrument to satisfy the mind's desire for music. The human eye
is an instrument to satisfy the mind's desire to view the created world.
Every other qualia follows the same pattern. Consciousness created the

sense of touch in order to feel the created world, the sense of hearing to hear the created world, and so on.

Religion often emerges as the repository of irrational mythmaking. But the Biblical creation story gets one crucial thing right. God entered his creation in order to enjoy it. We are told that Adam and Eve "heard the sound of the Lord God as he was walking in the garden in the cool of the day" (Genesis 3:8). In modern terms, we'd say that consciousness permeates the world. Sight, sound, and all other qualities arose so that the universal mind could experience itself.

Religion got something else right that was crucial: There are no limitations on the creative process. Reality is as malleable as a dream. If you forget this, reality starts to freeze up, and then it's only a small step to a world so rigid and self-enclosed that every other dimension is excluded. A classic example arose when the Church denounced Galileo for heresy because he espoused the notion that the Earth moves around the Sun, in contrast to the Church's geocentric view, in which the Earth is the immobile center of the universe. Brought before the Inquisition in 1633, the judges "forced him under the threat of torture to kneel and read aloud a long, abject retraction saying that he 'abjured, cursed, and detested' the heliocentric theory." (Legend has it, probably incorrectly, that as he rose to his feet, he muttered the words *eppur si muove . . .* , meaning, "and yet it does move . . .")

Physicist David Deutsch relates Galileo's ordeal, as every scientist does, as a victory for direct observation of the heavens. It offended faith to second-guess God's works with mathematical calculations. In the long run, the great age of science was dawning. In the short run, Galileo was convicted and consigned to house arrest. Enough fear was created that science was suppressed in the Mediterranean basin for centuries, Deutsch tells us. But he makes a crucial concession here.

Given that the Inquisition believed in divine revelation, Deutsch says, "their world-view was false, but it was not illogical." One kind of observation, such as Galileo's, could not limit God. "As they would put it, God could produce the same observed effects in an infinity of differ-ent ways." Galileo's theory about the sun and the planets was arrogant if it claimed to be "a way of knowing, through one's own fallible obser-vation and reason, which way He chose." God's way is infinite; man's way is finite.

The language of Church authority is obnoxious to a scientist, but hidden inside the judgment against Galileo is one of the essential points of Eastern wisdom traditions. The visible world is a world only of appearances. Looking at appearances doesn't tell you what creation is actually like. (Even the Earth going around the Sun turns out to be only an appearance. If you stand at the edge of the Milky Way, the whole solar system is orbiting around the galaxy. If you stand at the starting point of the Big Bang, the Milky Way is rushing away from every other galaxy as the universe expands, taking Earth with it. Indeed, Earth's motion can be described from infinite perspectives, just as the Inquisi-tion claimed.) The ancient Vedic seers put this in terms of *maya*, which means more than illusion. Maya is a goddess whose seductive charm tempts the mind into believing that the unreal is actually real. Nothing she shows us is trustworthy. We are so distracted by the spectacle of life that we forget who created it, ourselves. We must place our trust in the creative process.

Then God matters, more than anything in creation, because *God* is the word we apply to the source of creation. It isn't necessary to worship the source, although reverence is certainly deserved if we want to give it. The necessary thing is to connect. Across the gap in the transcendent world are some totally necessary things that cannot be created, not by hand, by imagination, or by thought.

What God Actually Is

Aspects of the transcendent world

Pure awareness
Pure intelligence
Pure creativity
Infinite potential
Unbounded possibilities
Bliss
Self-organization
Infinite correlation
All matter and energy in a virtual state

These are the best terms the mind can devise when looking at Oneness from across the gap. The list doesn't imply anything religious; it applies strictly to consciousness and how it operates. Consciousness is creative and intelligent. It can correlate a quadrillion brain connections or the fifty processes that a liver cell performs. It can keep track of simultaneous activities at the same time (allowing you to breathe, digest, walk, be pregnant, think about your baby, and feel happy at the same time).

You are finding God whenever any of these aspects begins to expand. God enters everyday life this way. When you experience greater creativity, you are inspired, which means "bringing in spirit." It doesn't matter if your inspiration is to make cookies, while Michelangelo's was to paint the ceiling of the Sistine Chapel. In both cases, an aspect of God, pure creativity, has been brought into the material world. The inspiration of a saint comes from the same source. When Saint Francis of Assisi says, "If God can work through me, he can work through anyone," he is uttering the truth about how pure consciousness enters the world: through each of us. No one is bound to the same creative path. Saint Francis chose to fashion his experience along the lines of humility, celibacy, charity, and devotion. Michelangelo chose art, beauty, nobility, and grandeur. These are all qualia, and so are the ingredients that go into all experiences.

But if you look at the list again, the items on it are not qualia. They are more basic than any experience. Existence itself depends upon them. Without intelligence, nothing would ever be understandable. Without creativity, nothing would ever be new. Without organizing power, everything would remain in a state of chaos. The one aspect of God that looks out of place is bliss. Isn't bliss the experience of happiness, which is much less than divine? But when used by Buddhists and the Vedic sages who preceded them, bliss (*Ananda*) is the vibrancy of creation, the underlying dynamism that enters the world as vitality, desire, ecstasy, and joy.

So, did you create that big black dog running toward you? Yes. Not "you" as an individual but "you" as an agent of consciousness itself. Clinging to individuality creates confusion here. A wave can lap at the White Cliffs of Dover and ask, "Did I create this magnificence?" Yes and no. The ocean washed away the shore; each wave played its part. You have always been universal, and to see yourself otherwise would be unreal. This is made clear in another Vedic image. When an ocean wave rises up, it says to itself, "I am a separate individual," but when it falls back, it says, "I am the ocean." As a creator, you rise up from the ocean of consciousness to create your personal reality. When you go deep inside, however, you see that you belong to the ocean of consciousness. It is creating reality through you without ever leaving the transcendent world.

In the end, to know God is to remember and to forget. You forget the illusion that you are separate, isolated, powerless, and stranded in an overwhelming cosmos. You remember that you are the dreamer who is in charge of the dream. What you perceive through the five senses isn't the same as reality. Go beyond the shadow play of appearances, and reality will greet you, as Rumi says, in "a world too full to talk about." Enter the realm of all possibilities. Making them come true is a great gift. It comes directly from God.

The Toughest Question

When you fully remember who you are, you become one with God. An invisible grace permeates every aspect of your life. The hope expressed in Psalm 23, "Surely goodness and mercy shall follow me all the days of my life," comes true. You cannot achieve such a state of grace overnight. You and I, wherever we find ourselves, must balance hope, faith, and knowledge. It's a precarious balance. There may be moments of grace that break through like sunshine through clouds. These moments don't come every day, however, unlike the personal trials that we face. The trick is to begin looking for the grace hidden beneath the struggle, and then your trials start to ease and fade away.

I want to show that spirituality can be a way of life at every stage of the path. At the beginning—and well into the middle—"the courage to be" means the courage to be confused. God seems relevant off and on. The possibility of finding peace or trusting in a higher power flickers. The rest of the time God is nowhere. Are these glimmers of the divine enough? Obviously not. When you watch the evening news, you will see some fresh disaster—a jetliner crashing into the Atlantic, genocide in the Congo, a gunman on the rampage in a movie theater who then shoots himself—pulling you back into the "real world." Your old conditioning kicks in: You believe the world is full of violence and chaos, and you have no choice but to meet it on its own terms, struggling to hold your own.

It takes a hidden element to keep us from backsliding into our old ingrained reactions. That element is wholeness. Unknown to us, wholeness is in charge of our lives. It keeps chaos at bay. It provides support even when bad things are happening. The world's wisdom traditions have an axiom: "As it is in the great, so it is in the small." In other words, even the tiniest fragment of reality *is* the whole. But you and I cling to the perspective of a fragment. Taking this point of view, no one can see wholeness. The air in a party balloon would be surprised to hear that there is no difference between it and the Earth's atmosphere. Until the balloon is popped, a thin membrane keeps it from knowing who it really is.

For you and me, the thin membrane is mental. From the perspective of a fragment, you approach your life as "I," a single, isolated person. This "I" possesses individual drives and motives. It wants more for itself. It thinks that consciousness is private. Looking out for number one, along with immediate family, takes top priority. But no matter how strong "I" becomes, outside forces are far more powerful, which makes existence insecure. God has the perspective of wholeness. At the end of the spiritual journey, the seeker who has become enlightened has also gained this perspective. He can say *Aham Brahmasmi*, "I am the universe," which is like seeing infinity in all directions, with no boundaries or limitations.

Mystery swirls around this word *enlightenment*, what it means and how to get there. Stripped of mystery, you are enlightened when you become completely self-aware. Each step on the spiritual path expands the self-awareness you started with. Your sense of self changes. You begin to perceive that wholeness is possible. (To lift an image from the Vedic tradition, you smell the sea even before you reach it.)

If you observe the following changes in yourself, wholeness is actually dawning.

Becoming Whole

How the path changes you

You feel less isolated, more connected to everything around you.

Insecurity is replaced with a sense of safety.

You realize that you belong.

The demands of "I, me, and mine" are not so strong.

You can see from a wider perspective than self-interest.

You act on the impulse to help and serve.

Life and death merge into a single cycle. Creation and destruction are no longer frightening.

Us-versus-them fades away. Divisions seem less meaningful.

Status and power become less important.

The ups and downs of everyday life don't trigger you as much.

You feel guided in your actions. Life is no longer random and full of impending crises.

You feel more balanced and at peace with yourself.

Being whole is a state that grows inside you, but reality has always been whole. The entire universe conspires to bring about every moment in time. In Sanskrit this fact is compressed in the verb *dhar*, "to uphold." Reality upholds itself and all the fragments that seem to exist in it. The fragmentation that is so obvious in the material world is maya, a part of the illusion. Gazing at billions of galaxies masks the reality that they all came from one event, a Big Bang that had no fragments. This is easy to understand now that physics has traced all matter and energy back to their source. But the mind has no Big Bang to refer to. Thinking is always fragmented. It takes place one thought at a time, so makes it much harder to see that all thoughts come from one mind. "My" mind is the most convincing fragment of all.

If you tell someone to stop clinging to the notion of "my" mind, they'll look alarmed and say, "You want me to lose my mind?" No, you want them to gain cosmic mind instead. It helps to substitute something you can actually see: your body. While you are focused on doing something small and specific—reading these words—fifty trillion cells are upholding that tiny action. Cells are not fooled by their isolated situation as individuals. They operate from wholeness all the time. Each is leading a spiritual life that any saint would envy.

Every cell follows a higher purpose, maintaining the whole body.
Each cell knows its place in the body. It has total security.
The body protects and embraces the life of every cell.
Without judgment or prejudice, every cell is accepted.
Every cell lives in the moment, constantly renewed, never clinging
to the old and outworn.
The natural flow of life is trusted to operate with supreme efficiency.
Individual cells are born and die, yet this all takes place against the
body's perfect balance.

None of these things are spiritual aspirations; they are facts of daily existence at the level of your cells. Everything that seems unreachable in spiritual terms—perfect surrender, humility, innocence, nonviolence, reverence for life—has been built into you. It doesn't matter how minuscule a single red blood corpuscle is; the wisdom of life upholds it.

This leads to a surprising conclusion. For a cell to remain alive, it depends upon infinity. A single cell can say *Aham Brahmasmi* without spending years in a cave in the Himalayas. Saying "I am the universe" doesn't mean that you are very, very big. The issue isn't about size, place, time, or space. It's about everything in creation being the same in essence, despite all appearances. Such differences, to use a Vedic image, are like a gold watch and a gold ring arguing over which one is more valuable. Trapped in their egos, they can't see that they are made of the same essence, which is gold. Brain cells exhibit intelligence. Is intelligence big or small? Would you need a lunch sack to carry it around in or a shipping container? The question is meaningless. Intelligence has no physical size. All the invisible attributes that uphold life have no physical size. The beauty of the spiritual path is that you are supported by an infinite power every step of the way.

The real issue is how much of infinity you can absorb into your life. When expansion is infinite, the whole project feels daunting. Why challenge your boundaries, which feel like home? You might go flying outward like a paddleball, only to come springing back on a rubber band. A liver or heart cell is fortunate. To remain alive, it must connect with wholeness. It cannot doubt or opt out, turn its back on its creator, or denounce God as a delusion. But you are even more fortunate. You have self-awareness, the ability to know who you are. So your spiritual path comes down to choosing an identity. You act like an isolated individual or like the whole. You either align yourself with the universe or you don't.

Alignment = self-acceptance, flow, balance, orderliness, being at peace

Nonalignment = self-judgment, suffering, struggle, opposition, restlessness, disorder

If you focus on the right side of the equation, life looks incredibly complicated. Paralyzed by a welter of choices, you'd hardly be able to start the car. At any given moment, you'd be deciding whether to accept or resist, to struggle or let go. Perhaps that's why we can't stop fantasizing about perfection. If you can only get the perfect body, the perfect house, the perfect mate, you will escape the hardest thing in life, which is ambivalence. All bodies, houses, and mates have imperfections. There are good days and bad. Love can unexpectedly turn into boredom or even hate.

The left side of each equation, however, consists of only one word.

You face only a single choice: to align yourself with wholeness or not. Simplicity is extremely powerful. You ask God to uphold you, and everything else follows. This is the holistic solution to all problems.

Many pages ago I mentioned how impossible it was to live as Jesus taught in the Sermon on the Mount. The lilies of the field do not toil or spin, but human beings spend a lifetime of toil. Jesus was holding out the same holistic solution that we have arrived at: Providence will uphold you when you are totally aligned with God, as nature upholds all simpler life-forms. "Look at the birds of the air; they neither sow nor reap nor gather into barns, and yet your heavenly Father feeds them. Are you not of more value than they? And can any of you by worrying add a single hour to your span of life?" (Matthew 6:26–27). The expression may be poetic, but the logic is pure wisdom: Alignment is the natural way; nonalignment isn't.

The five "poisons"

It's hard to be left behind, but that's the situation we all find ourselves in. If we could be sitting at the feet of Jesus, Buddha, or one of the great Vedic rishis, they would show us, day by day, when we were aligned with God and when we weren't. The New Testament swings constantly between the master's rebukes and his praise. At one moment, Jesus scorns his followers for demanding healings and miracles. At another moment, he bestows healings and miracles with a smile. It must have been incredibly confusing for them. Caught between rebuke and blessing, the disciples needed constant course correction.

You and I need course correction just as much, with only ourselves to follow. The obstacles that we face test our faith and tease us with hope that soon fades. It's necessary, then, to examine the broken state we've created. Nonalignment has been a way of life for generations. (What greater symptom of our plight than the doctrine of a random, cold, uncaring universe that Dawkins and company promote?) The Vedic masters point to five obstacles that keep us out of alignment with God. The Sanskrit term for these obstacles is more dramatic: *klesha,* which literally means "poison." The five poisons are

- Ignorance (the inability to tell the real from the false)
- Egoism (identifying with "me," the individual self)
- Attachment (clinging to certain things, the objects of desire)
- Aversion (rejecting other things, the objects of revulsion)
- Fear of death

The first poison starts a chain reaction, we might say, leading to the last. Fear of death, the fifth *klesha,* is the end product on the assembly line of ignorance. Not many people are happy to be told that they've shaped their lives through ignorance; it sounds offensive. A more palatable way is to talk about fragmentation.

How did you come to see yourself as a fragment? The first step was forgetfulness. A rich man afflicted with amnesia forgets his bank account. The money is still there, but forgetfulness makes him impoverished. You and I lost the memory of wholeness. We are still whole, but we've lost the advantage of it. The chain reaction has started.

> You forget that you are whole.
> You see yourself as "I," an isolated, vulnerable fragment.
> "I" has desires that it clings to in order to feel safer.
> It also has things that feel threatening, which it pushes away.
> Despite its pursuit of desire, "I" knows that it will die one day, and this knowledge makes it very afraid.

The five poisons look bad, yet one thing gives hope: Once you extract the first poison—forgetting who you are—the chain reaction stops. This is an invaluable secret. People waste years trying to improve the bits and pieces of their lives. Let's say you look in the mirror one day and dislike the body you see. You want to impress the opposite sex, so you resolve to exercise. Running on a treadmill stokes desire by leading to better fitness; it stokes revulsion by being boring and tiring. You pay for an expensive date, which stokes the desire to be considered a success, but knowing that you are compensating for your insecurity stokes revulsion. You have been poisoned by the *kleshas* of attachment and revulsion. The result is that "I" feels conflicted, falls back on inertia, and winds up feeling worse about itself because it has failed to get what it wanted—a better body. The whole process takes place in consciousness, as clinging, revulsion, desire, and ego clash in a confusing melee. But there was never any real hope in the first place. By trying to satisfy "I," you were trying to placate an illusion.

The way out of this dilemma is to remember who you really are, which means aligning yourself with what is real. Instead of asking "What would Jesus do?" which seems pretty imaginary, ask "What would my real self do?" That question is more authentic and immediate.

Your real self would take responsibility for the reflection that the universe sends. Reality is a mirror that never lies.

Your real self would focus on inner growth. It wants nothing more than to reach its full potential.

Your real self wouldn't project blame and judgment on others.

Your real self wouldn't act on impulse. It relies on self-reflection. It makes decisions in a state of calm, away from the chaos.

You might grumble that you still see a flabby body in the mirror.

Actually not, because once you inhabit your real self, judgment ends; focusing on externals ends; you are no longer motivated by insecurity, which traps people on the endless treadmill of self-improvement. This is just a broad outline, but it's enough to show you that "I" has a very different agenda from your real self.

God should be a way of life that you can rely upon as securely as you rely upon grocery stores, a monthly paycheck, and your insurance policy. What would be the point of an unreliable God? The devout French writer Simone Weil put it this way: "In what concerns divine things, belief is not appropriate. Only certainty will do. Anything less than certainty is unworthy of God." I totally agree, but we need a process that arrives at certainty. Let's set aside absolute answers—they leave no middle ground, no evolution, and no chance to correct your mistakes. Unbending certainty is the position taken by atheists at one extreme and fundamentalists at the other. For the rest of us, certainty grows from inner experience, and this unfoldment takes time. Meanwhile, we have a whole life to live, and we must embrace our uncertainty. It's okay to be wobbly as long as you are still heading down the right road.

The toughest question

No one has really been left behind. As a child, I didn't know this. I marveled at the miracles that Jesus performed in the New Testament—my early schooling took place under Christian Brothers, mostly Irish missionaries who ran the best schools in India. But Jesus's miracles weren't anything I'd ever see. Walking on water has gone away. A process of disenchantment began, and it was easy for me to slide from disenchantment to disillusionment, then on to amnesia, forgetting that my childhood ideals ever existed. The best I could do was adapt to a world devoid of God. If he would not intervene in the world's evils, I would. I think many doctors follow this path in their own way. What I didn't see was that the entire slide perfectly matched the five *kleshas*.

If you find yourself fighting the world's many evils, you are immersed in them. The system of evil has claimed you. It sounds shocking, but if you believe in evil, you have forgotten who you really are. I thought helping sick people would improve one small corner of the world. From a wider perspective, though, I was doing something quite different. I was keeping an illusion going. Every time you fight evil, you are reinforcing the system of evil, which would shrink away unless people paid attention to it.

Krishnamurti was one of the frankest teachers on this point, regardless of how it baffled people or hurt their feelings. In one of his journals, he recounts an incident in India when a kindly, well-dressed woman came asking for a contribution to her cause, the prevention of cruelty to animals.

"What's the reason for this cause?" Krishnamurti asked.

"Animals are terribly mistreated in this country," the woman said. "I know that you teach Ahimsa, reverence for life. Surely this means being kind to animals."

"I meant, why is this your cause? What's your reason for taking it up?" Krishnamurti replied.

The woman was taken aback. "I feel how much these poor creatures suffer."

"Then it's your own distress you want to alleviate," said Krishnamurti. "There is a way. Look deep into yourself. Where is the seed of violence? If animals are being mistreated, it is because we don't take responsibility for our own violence. The seed is nowhere else but in you."

The wider perspective can be very painful. It rips away the ego's pride in being right and good. Krishnamurti doesn't recount whether he made a contribution or not. (He probably did, being a supporter of good causes.) His aim was to expose the root of evil itself, because that is the only way to end it once and for all. The same applies to any particular evil one can name. Imagine that a psychic reads your mind and tells you, "Your notion of true evil is child abuse, domestic violence, religious hatred, and a helpless person dying in horrible pain from cancer." You might agree with this list—surely most people would—and yet it implies no solution. You can give to good causes that help victims of child abuse and support harsher laws against domestic violence. You can pray that you don't die in agony from incurable cancer. But these acts only skirt the question; they don't get at evil itself.

The question of evil is the toughest we can ask and the greatest challenge to God. Why does evil exist? Why doesn't God intervene? If the evils we deplore in society are symptoms of cosmic evil, then hope vanishes. The entire spiritual enterprise collapses, as it did for countless people after the Gulag, the Holocaust, and the atomic bombing of Hiroshima and Nagasaki. Although carried out by human beings, these horrors felt satanic. They erased any optimism that good could triumph over evil. The ultimate reason to despair, as many saw it, was that the perpetrators who perform the most evil acts in modern history thought of themselves as moral and their victims as the actual bad people.

If we can answer the toughest question, the whole trend reverses. Once evil is exposed as an illusion, reality has a chance to convince us. Love can prove itself more powerful than fear. The greatest of spiritual ideals, a world free of evil, will begin to actualize. On the other hand, if evil cannot be defeated, it will doom the spiritual path itself.

"Do you want everything to be good?"

If you are spiritual, does that provide a safeguard against the heinous crimes perpetrated on humanity? We can't begin at such an extreme with questions about cosmic evil and that dark, seductive creature Satan. Instead, we have a more modest way to get at the question of evil. Start with a personal question: "Would you accept a world that contained no badness at all? Do you want everything to be good?"

Your immediate answer might be yes. For instance, pain is the body's idea of evil, and a world without physical pain sounds desirable. But a handful of patients worldwide have a rare condition (traced to two mutations in the SCN9A gene) that prevents them from feeling any pain. Justin Heckert, a journalist who was reporting on a thirteen-year-old girl living with this anomaly, writes that:

> She really has a lot less fear and regard for her body than other girls her age, anyone her age, anyone at all, really. She was playing air hockey with her sister so crazily I thought she might hurt herself, or hurt her sister. She threw half of her body onto the table and was trying to smash the puck toward the little goal as hard as she could. Her parents were mortified.

But Heckert quickly lost his envy of a child who felt no pain, accepting instead what her doctor said: "Pain is a gift that she doesn't have." In grade school a monitor followed her constantly to make sure she wasn't injured; after every recess it was necessary to check her eyes in case grit had gotten in. At home, her parents "got rid of all their furniture with sharp corners. They laid down the softest carpet they could find. They didn't let [their daughter] roller-skate. They didn't let her ride a bicycle. They wrapped her arms in layers of gauze to keep her from rubbing them raw. They used a baby monitor in her bedroom to listen for grinding teeth."

Pain is a gift, once you realize the consequences of doing without it. Fire burns the skin, but it also cooks food. Then what about violence? A world without crime and war seems completely desirable, but surgery is a form of controlled violence. The body is (carefully) torn open, exposing it to many risks. A healthy ecosystem depends on one species eating another, which entails violence. Make all animals vegetarians, and in the absence of predators, nothing would stop insects from filling the world; they already outweigh all mammals many times over.

And what about mental suffering, which is entangled with shame, guilt, fear, and anger? Two angry factions in a civil war wind up killing each other and many innocent bystanders. On the face of it, anger has led to great evil. But the combatants don't stop, because their desire for vengeance makes them accept anger as justified and even righteous. Civil wars are driven by desires—defending your home, hatred of "the other," racial and religious intolerance—that are just as tied to anger as revenge. War glorifies anger, masking the suffering that it brings. Caught up in a righteous cause, a soldier might brush aside his own suffering, but once the war is over, new forms of mental suffering emerge, such as guilt and the complex symptoms of post-traumatic stress disorder.

Mental suffering can't be summarized in a few paragraphs. Let's stick to our original line of questioning: "Do you want everything to be good? Is a painless world desirable?" If you define mental pain as depression, anxiety, schizophrenia, and other mental disorders, no one wants them to exist. But the need for pain applies to the mental world, too. Fear keeps you from putting your hand in the fire a second time. Guilt teaches children not to steal from the cookie jar even when their mothers aren't watching. Mental pain is useful in all kinds of ways when it isn't excessive.

What we call evil is often something we can't do without and don't want to. Human beings thrive on contrast. Without pain there can be no pleasure, only a bland state of nonstimulation. (Hence the natural suspicion that young children show when they are told about heaven—it sounds boring to sit on clouds and play harps for eternity.) Are we designed to be good in the first place? Apparently so. Researchers into infant behavior have found that babies as young as four months old will try to pick up an object that their mothers dropped and hand it back.

But the impulse to goodness is mixed in with contrary impulses. Other researchers have found that young children learn to act the way their parents tell them to; they know what "be good" means in terms of getting approval at home. But when left alone without an adult in preschool, the same child may suddenly turn from Jekyll to Hyde, snatching toys from other children and showing no remorse when their victims cry. Still, these intriguing findings don't solve the problem of evil itself. For that, we must go deeper.

In duality, everything inevitably has its opposite. Good cannot be separated from evil, just as light cannot be separated from darkness. They are inseparable, one of the basic teachings in Buddhism. Every golden age in mythology has led to a fall. Paradise always has a flaw, if not a serpent in the garden, because our divided nature demands it. Should God be held responsible for our predicament? Or is evil entirely a product of human nature?

Satan and the shadow

It's hard for God to escape responsibility for evil. You can do it by fiat—simply declaring that God is all goodness. Many believers do just that, assigning the evil part of creation to a cosmic demon, who was given the name Satan in Hebrew, meaning "the adversary." Regardless of whether this arch-demon is a fallen angel, once you assign evil to Satan—leaving aside the existence of hell, the kingdom that he rules—God gets demoted. An omnipotent God wouldn't have an enemy who holds sway over us almost as powerfully as God himself. A loving God wouldn't let the Devil hurt us all the time. An omniscient God would know when the Devil is going to strike and would intervene, or at the very least give us advance warning. Once God loses his monopoly over love, power, and wisdom, trouble is afoot.

To allow God to be God in all his glory, religion shifted the blame for evil. It became a human problem, tied in with temptation and sin. Adam and Eve had every other food laid out before them, but they perversely ate the apple. Perversity has struck with us. So God permits evil to exist because we deserve it. We run loose with desire; our aggression makes us attack and kill one another. We erect moral schemes only to defy them at will, act like hypocrites, and turn to crime and rebellion.

Shifting the blame resulted in a huge burden, but most people are willing to carry it. Some evils arise beyond our control, such as hurricanes and other natural disasters. Others are the product of genes, like cancer, but even here blame persists. Poor lifestyle choices are connected to many cancers, and even if they weren't, patients anxiously ask themselves, "Did I cause my disease?" As for natural disasters, we've all become aware of the human contribution to global warming and the erratic weather it has produced.

The two schemes, cosmic evil and human evil, merge in the concept of the shadow, which manages to be universal and human at the same time. No one ever doubted that darkness lurks in the human heart. But modern psychology wanted a systematic, rational way to understand this darkness; the early Swiss psychoanalyst C. G. Jung provided it when he described a force in the unconscious he named "the shadow." To the domain of the shadow, Jung consigned guilt, shame, anger, and anxiety. But the shadow is more than a warehouse for negative impulses. Being conscious, it looks at the world through its own distorted lens, and when it does, anger and fear seem justified. The shadow makes us want to kill our enemies and feel good about it, or at least justified.

The shadow sends messages to the rest of the psyche that are no doubt powerful, contradicting the desire for goodness, well-being, and happiness. It persuades us that anger, which feels good at the time, *is* good. Never mind the aftermath. To use Jung's phrase, the shadow creates "the fog of illusion" that surrounds everyone. Since there is no escape from it, the shadow is universal. I once debated a staunch Jungian who argued that peace can never be achieved because Mars, the archetype of war, resides permanently in our psyches. (So does sex, I argued back, but people don't run around in a state of erotic mania. Primitive drives leave room for choice, the domain of the higher brain.) In the depths of the unconscious, Satan and the shadow join hands. Each is equally invisible, equally a projection of the mind.

If cosmic evil holds such sway that even God permits it to exist, what hope do we have of undoing it? This question was tested in the Book of Job, which some scholarly accounts say was the last part of the Hebrew Bible to be written, but the same themes are found in more ancient texts from Sumer and Egypt (giving support to Jung's notion that mythology from all cultures can be traced to the same archetypal roots). In the Book of Job, God and Satan wager over the soul of a man in the land of Uz. God's adversary claims that he can tempt any man to renounce God, even the most righteous. God claims that Job, being of utmost righteousness, cannot be swayed. He gives Satan a free hand to torment Job, the only restriction being that he cannot kill him.

The wager intrigues any reader the first time he encounters the story. What kind of torture will Satan inflict? Will Job hold out or give in? The makings of an exciting morality play are all there. As it turns out, the afflictions of Job cover almost every form of human suffering. He loses everything that was good in his life—money, crops, wife, and children. His body is covered with seeping sores. The infamous three friends appear to tell Job why God has done these horrible things to him. Their basic argument is that he deserves everything that has befallen him. As their taunts and blame increase, the setup makes us sympathize more with the victim. No convincing reason is given for why a good man should suffer so much. There couldn't be a reason, in fact, since Job and his friends have no clue that God and Satan are using him as a pawn in a cosmic bet.

If you are literal-minded, the bet was cruel to begin with. A God who uses souls like poker chips isn't worth worshiping. Besides, if God can keep Satan from killing Job, he should be able to keep Satan from hurting him in any way short of death. True goodness doesn't say, "Okay, you can be evil, only don't go too far."

So Job's tale has to be read as an allegory. The cosmic wager stands for the mystery of evil, which descends upon our lives without reason, and when it does, our suffering feels undeserved. Clearly, despite the three friends accusing him of hypocrisy and hidden sin, Job doesn't deserve his afflictions. The allegory needs a moral, and the Book of Job has one that is quite unconvincing.

A young servant named Elihu has been listening to the argument between Job and his friends with increasing dismay. Jumping to his feet, he startles everyone by speaking in a holy voice, as God's stand-in. Both sides are wrong, Elihu declares. The three friends are wrong to claim that Job has a hidden flaw that God is punishing. Job is wrong to believe that his righteous life trumps God's power. God can do what he wants, when he wants, to whomever he wants. His ways do not have to be justified to man.

The three friends flee, their hypocrisy and disloyalty exposed. Job's reaction isn't clear, but a happy ending is tacked on (probably by later scribes; the whole framework of a cosmic wager also seems to be a late addition). He is healed, and his wealth is restored. A new wife gives birth to sons to replace those who died. Righteousness has prevailed. Job never renounced God, and having won the wager, God rewards his favored child. But the Job who emerges safe and sound from his horrendous trials isn't the same Job as before. Addressing God, he says, "I have heard of thee by the hearing of the ear: but now mine eye seeth thee. Wherefore I abhor *myself*, and repent in dust and ashes" (Job 42:5–6).

He has become humble and repentant—a default position frequently reinforced in the Hebrew Bible—but this seems strange. Job wasn't proud or boastful to begin with. He was the model devotee of God. The allegory is telling us something deeper. Before his trials, Job thought he understood God "by the hearing of the ear"—sermons, the reading of the Torah, temple rituals, the teachings of elder rabbis. All of this pointed in the wrong direction. God isn't the same as talk about God. When Job declares that he abhors himself, he is referring to the arrogant ego, which would demote God to just another thing to be figured out and managed.

For me, this is a profound story about the *kleshas,* the poisons that distort reality. Job, for all his goodness, is attached to his own righteousness. He has turned his existence into a regimen dictated by scripture and the law. Such a life is unreal when there is no contact with the transcendent world. Rules about God are like rules about driving a car. They can prevent mishaps and keep everyone safer, but passing a DMV exam isn't the same as driving down the highway. Reality can't be defined by rules and laws. It is dynamic, unbounded, creative, all-embracing, and eternal.

The allegory of Job applies to the bad things in our lives. Pain and suffering weaken faith; God gets deposed with every new atrocity on the evening news. But what topples is only an image. God himself isn't even touched by bad things; afflictions are part of the illusion. In a whimsical moment, when I came across a Twitter argument over whether heaven is real, I tweeted, "Material existence is an illusion. Heaven is an upgrade of the illusion." That's why Satan, as Job's tormentor, is given free rein in the world of appearances, while God, who abides in the transcendent, doesn't interfere. God's role isn't to upgrade the illusion but to lead us out of it.

Evil in a vacuum

Even though we might dissect evil into a thousand parts, we don't need to. Escaping evil is far more important than explaining it. Find your true self, and you will no longer want to participate in the illusion.

You will create a personal reality that isn't tied to the play of opposites. At that point, Job's lesson becomes abundantly clear. Don't be attached to your own goodness or someone else's badness. Find out your real relationship to God, and base your life on that.

Your real relationship with God emerges by eliminating everything that led to a false relationship.

You and God

When the relationship goes bad

You lose your connection to God whenever you

Fear divine punishment
Feel burdened by God's demands
Reduce God to a set of dos and don'ts
Defend God with anger or violence
Shirk responsibility by saying that something is God's will
Despair that God has turned against you
Hope to be so good that God can't help but love you
Keep guilty and shameful secrets
Live as if God is secondary to the "real" world
Treat other people as if God loves them less or not at all

These ingredients don't just sour your relationship with God; they'd doom any relationship between you and another person. Living in fear, keeping secrets, using anger and violence—no positive relationship can grow under those conditions, even if it manages to limp along. When applied to your relationship to God, the effect is more disastrous. Evil is created in the misplaced desire to make ourselves worthy of God. Holy wars are the most obvious example, but guilt, shame, and anger are direct results of an either/or trap that is inescapable: either you aren't good enough for God, or no matter how good you are, God doesn't care. Suffering is rooted in a false relationship to God, and when we suffer, we lash out at ourselves and others. When Emerson wrote that evil is the absence of good, he didn't satisfy those who believe in Satan, an active agent for evil. But what Emerson meant turns on the word *privation* or lack.

> Evil is merely privative, not absolute: it is like cold, which is
> the privation of heat. All evil is so much death or nonentity . . .
> Benevolence is absolute and real.

This remark echoes the world's wisdom traditions, which say that evil is like a vacuum, the emptiness of illusion. Fill the vacuum with reality, and evil vanishes. I'm not talking about a magic trick that makes genocide, war crimes, and oppression go away overnight. Human nature does its worst when it finds no way to change. But you will undergo an inner transformation, and as you do, the labels of good and evil won't be as sticky. The fullness of God will steadily fill the vacuum. You are creeping out of the illusion, quietly and without flashiness.

Let me give a sense of the stages that mark this transformation.

Fading in the Light

As consciousness grows, evil shrinks

Stage 1: Fear

When consciousness is dominated by fear and insecurity, evil is everywhere. It comes in physical threats to our bodies, the struggle to provide food and shelter, and natural disasters that no one can prevent. God offers no protection. The only protection is self-defense.

Stage 2: Ego

Ego brings the building of a strong self. "I" can stand up to challenges. Living a good life, obeying the rules, and trusting that God is fair will keep bad things at bay. In a world of risk and reward overseen by God, "I" will be blessed for my goodness as long as I avoid the pitfalls of sin.

Stage 3: Social order

Individual consciousness expands to include others. The group bonds together for the common good. A system of laws protects people from crime and other wrongdoing, enforced by the police. The greatest bond is a shared version of God. Faith sustains the belief that evil can never defeat God's love for his children.

Stage 4: Empathy and understanding

Consciousness expands to embrace the world "in here." One sees that other people have their own motives and beliefs, just as you do. They share your feelings, as you share theirs. It becomes possible to understand why people behave as they do. The seed of evil isn't just inside "bad people" but in everyone. God, who understands everyone, is forgiving. He embraces the wrongdoer and the righteous alike.

Stage 5: Self-discovery

Consciousness expands to ask why. Why do we act the way we do? What are the roots of good and bad in human life? There is no longer pure evil or cosmic evil. The responsibility lies squarely on us. By trusting in reason and insight, we can explore our nature and improve it. God is clarity, the light of reason, no longer judging us. He wants us to live in the light.

Stage 6: Compassion

Consciousness expands to love humanity. The wall between right and wrong has crumbled. All people are valued no matter how they behave. God looks down on his children with love. Knowing that love is eternal, people can offer compassion, treating others as God would treat them.

Stage 7: Being

Consciousness expands beyond duality. The play of good and evil is allowed to be what it is. One's allegiance has shifted elsewhere. Having sensed the transcendent world, one enters it and lives there. God is One. Merging with pure being, a person lives in a state of grace, which holds the ultimate power for overcoming evil.

As a person passes through these seven stages, evil changes. It moves from being an overwhelming threat to being a minor threat and then no threat at all. When you try to figure out why evil exists, you may decide that the source is a cosmic demon, a flaw in human nature, or a shadowy domain that has its own agenda. But the bottom line is the same. Evil is *created*. You can fight as hard against it as you want. In the end, the solution doesn't exist on the level of the created. Emerson intuited this, I think, when he said that evil is temporary. Anything that depends on human perception can't be eternal. The only eternal state is Being, the simplest state of existence. Plant your feet there; it is the only safe haven, where evil has no meaning.

The power of Being

As a boy in India, I imbibed faith from my mother, who was very devout. I stood beside her every day as she lit incense and prayed before the household altar. Afternoons were frequently filled with the sounds of *kirtan*, group singing of devotional songs that were fervent and enchanting.

In the still of the night
From the darkness comes a light.
And I know in my heart it is you.

When the fire in my soul
Burns with longing for the goal.
Then I know in my heart it is you.

It didn't stay with me. Faith leaked away with each passing year. I was fortunate, stranded in Boston as a young doctor drinking after hours so that I would be accepted by the crowd, smoking to relieve stress, and driving myself to succeed. Nonetheless I felt the vacuum that exists when fullness is absent. I had witnessed lung cancer patients crossing the street as soon as they left my care, rushing to buy a pack of cigarettes at the corner convenience store. I had seen the look of abject fear in dying patients who were deprived of solace. The faith my mother introduced to me could have turned to cynicism or despair.

Looking back to childhood didn't change my life. I sensed my own emptiness and wanted to do something about it. Here a piece of good fortune came my way. The religion I had been taught didn't focus on sin, guilt, temptation, or the Devil. It makes no promise of a heavenly reward or punishment in hell. It helps to have that old lumber cleared away. The secret to finding God, it taught, is to fill yourself up with Being (capitalized to denote pure, absolute being). Once you do that, you know that you are nothing but Being, and in that knowledge comes total awakening. You look around and behold light in all directions.

Wherever you start from, waking up is the destination. Evil is the most powerful of illusions, supported by fear, the most powerful of negative emotions. Whenever you are in the grip of fear, a panicked voice inside screams, "Get away! Run! You're about to die." Fear constricts the mind. It freezes you up and blots out everything else. By contrast, what can Being do? Its voice is silent. It makes no demands. It doesn't tell you to choose A over B, because Being is beyond duality. People bitterly accuse God for not intervening in the world, yet Being has no other choice. It underlies everything equally—in that regard Hamlet was wrong. "To be or not to be" isn't a real choice. To be is inescapable. So Being is left to solve all problems without speaking, acting, changing, or interfering. Success doesn't look very probable, does it?

In the famous Beatles song, the advice to "let it be" is called "words of wisdom." I agree—nothing is wiser, because when Being becomes human, it isn't a passive state. It's a mode of living, one that most people have never tried. This book has outlined what this mode of living calls for, from showing generosity of spirit and expressing love to finding inner silence and following your own guidance.

What changed my life had nothing to do, in the end, with who I was as a person. The labels I attached to myself—*Indian physician, a success, well-loved, self-reliant,* and so on—were positive. Like heaven, the illusion I lived in came with upgrades. None of that actually mattered. What mattered was that I shifted into a new mode of living, beginning with an empty feeling inside and working from there to fill the vacuum. Saints and angels didn't light the way. Every day I did what I always did, getting up before dawn, making hospital rounds, and seeing a stream of patients in my private practice.

The difference was that I aligned myself with my Being. The verb *dhar,* "to uphold," leads to a way of life that the universe upholds, called dharma. Foreign words aren't better than common everyday words. Get to know yourself, and you will be in your dharma. Dharma comes down to one crucial thing: trusting Being to give you a course correction when you need it. Being provides hints about a higher reality. You feel subtly wrong when you veer into ego and selfishness. Being speaks silently, but existence is tilted in its favor. A few hidden advantages are tucked away in our lives.

Moving forward is favored over inertia.
Once it begins, evolution accelerates its pace.
Consciousness naturally expands.
The more you know yourself, the better your life becomes.
Positive intentions are supported more than negative intentions.
Individual consciousness is connected to God consciousness.

These advantages are subtle, but they endow Being with enormous power. When you think with love about your children, the thought is also occurring in God's mind—they both have the power to bless. If you are on your way to the movies and stop to help a traveler stranded in the snow, your impulse is the same as the impulse of salvation. The toughest questions will never stop plaguing the mind. God is the place where the mind finds an answer beyond thought. When you see this, no one in the world is an enemy, only a fellow traveler. The door to Being is open to everyone, leaving evil behind at the threshold.

Epilogue: God at a Glance

pproval is sweet. Anyone who wants it should avoid writing about God. No one will completely agree with you. (In a multicultural world, that's good.) You won't get the satisfaction of preaching to the choir—in most churches, the choir stalls are growing empty and cold. In a single week in 2013, the *New York Times* ran two op-ed pieces that denied the possibility of spiritual aspirations. One was titled "The Blessings of Atheism"; the other, "The Myth of Universal Love." They appeared right after Christmas. Perhaps that was the point. Being of good cheer left a bitter taste. God is a divider, not a uniter.

I've tried to present God without demanding an either/or choice. If the *Bhagavad Gita* is right to say, "All roads lead to me," meaning God, the road of nonbelief can't be judged against. I don't go to church or temple myself. The writer of "The Blessings of Atheism" decries people like me, who think of themselves as "spiritual but not religious." With undisguised disdain, she continues with this phrase, "as translated from the psychobabble, can mean just about anything—that the speaker is an atheist who fears social disapproval or a fence-sitter who wants the theoretical benefits of faith . . . without the obligations of actually practicing a religion."

Or it can mean something genuine. Atheism makes a mistake when it equates religious practice with spirituality. The deeper I got into this book, the clearer it became that almost anything one can say about God implies some kind of mistake. No one has a monopoly on the truth.

That doesn't mean that truth doesn't exist. In the same way, no matter how badly religions act, it doesn't prove that God doesn't exist. So many heated emotions swirl around God that I took the tack of meeting atheists on their own ground. Dawkins and company own a label maker that stamps their camp with approving words like *rational, scientific, sane, courageous,* and *logical.* When the label maker is pointed at anyone who believes in God, it spits out demeaning words—*irrational, superstitious, conformist, illogical,* and *crazy.*

Belief deserves its share of the good labels, so I apply *sanity, reason,* and *logic* to support the reality of God. Faith can't save itself. Stranded in a secular world, it will fall on deaf ears unless we talk in secular terms. In an ideal world, both sides would obey the injunction in the Old Testament to "be still and know that I am God." In our silence, we could take time to read Rumi, Kabir, and Tagore. God is in the thrill of inspired verse, as in this couplet:

> *Listen, my heart, to the whispering of the world.*
> *That is how it makes love to you.*

That's Tagore, and he doesn't have to mention God for you to feel that he is spiritual.

> *I grew tired of the road*
> *when it took me here and there.*
> *I married it in love*
> *when it took me Everywhere.*

Tagore again, just as spiritual, just as free of religiosity. A book that speaks entirely from the heart would be the next best thing to silence. When you have written a sentence that you're sure will convince a skeptic, you set yourself up for a fall. I've wept over verses that make another person snicker or look bored.

Which leaves the arena of ideas, where reason, sanity, and logic must be applied. With that in mind, I'll end by offering a batch of key ideas, those that must be addressed by both sides. Each idea points to a bigger discussion in the book. On their own, they are like telegrams, a few phrases to get the message across. I've divided the batch into three sections that correspond to the major subjects the text has covered: militant atheism, faith, and God. In my new enthusiasm for social media, I've tweeted these ideas, so I can attest that they generate heat, one way or another. What they can do here is better, I think. You have an opportunity to see where your beliefs have wound up.

Even your most cherished beliefs may have shifted—or not. We are often the worst judges of what is going on in our inner world. Ideas mostly play on the surface of the mind. It's better to rely on a poetic image about God. He is like a faint perfume detected when you are drowsing off at night. You hardly know what delicious scent awakens you, but for a while it's hard to go back to sleep again.

Militant Atheism

Ten Flaws in the Dawkins Delusion

1. His atheism attacks a Sunday school version of God as if there were no other. It lumps any kind of religious belief in with the excesses of extreme fanatics.

2. His atheism rests on the belief that the universe has no intelligent source. Yet a random universe is the least likely explanation for how intelligent life came about.

3. His atheism equates reality with the material world, as perceived by the five senses. This fails to account for the quantum revolution, which opened up reality far beyond the visible world.

4. His atheism traces all events back to inflexible laws of nature but

cannot explain why the laws of nature exist or where they came from.

5. His atheism uses evolution as an argument against an intelligent source for life, even though survival of the fittest cannot explain the creation of life.

6. His atheism positions itself as rational but cannot explain the source of rationality. How does random brain activity produce order and logic?

7. His atheism claims that biology is the basis of consciousness without offering a theory for how molecules learned to think.

8. His atheism views the brain in terms of rigid cause-and-effect. All thought and behavior is deterministic. He gives no explanation for free will, creativity, or insight.

9. His atheism denies the existence of the self, considering it an illusion created by the brain. Yet neuroscience has never found a location for "I" anywhere in the brain.

10. His atheism cannot explain how the illusory self arrives at self-knowledge.

Faith

Ten Reasons Why Faith Is Worthwhile

1. Faith is not blind belief but a knowing that comes from experience.
2. Faith is the willingness to step into the unknown.
3. Faith expresses wonder before the mystery of existence.
4. Faith comes from inner silence and what it reveals.
5. Faith brings trust in the inner world of insight, intuition, and imagination.
6. Faith brings a person closer to the source of creation.
7. Faith introduces the true self, which is beyond ego.

8. Faith connects the world "in here" with the world "out there."

9. Faith abolishes the divide between natural and supernatural.

10. Faith in your deepest self is faith in God.

God

Ten Ideas That Give God a Future

1. God is the intelligence that conceives, governs, constructs, and becomes the universe.

2. God is not a mythical person—he is Being itself.

3. God is uncreated. The universe cannot reveal God, since everything that exists is created.

4. God exists as a field of all possibilities.

5. God is pure consciousness, the source of all thoughts, feelings, and sensations.

6. God transcends all opposites, including good and evil, which arise in the field of duality.

7. God is One but diversifies into the many—he makes possible the observer, the observed, and the process of observation.

8. God is pure bliss, the source of every human joy.

9. God is the self of the universe.

10. There is only God. The universe is God made manifest.

Acknowledgments

A new book expresses itself as it grows, sometimes more from the brain than the heart, sometimes the reverse. First, I am deeply indebted to the many eminent scientists in the physical and biological sciences I have been dialoguing with over the last few years. They have broadened and strengthened my understanding in countless ways. This book on God grew from the need to make spirituality credible for modern people, walking them back from the brink of unbelief. I'm very grateful for the opportunity to fulfill this need, and to the people who worked with such dedication to make it happen.

The team at Harmony and Crown has stood by me and believed in my work through many changes in the publishing world. Tina Constable (publisher at Crown), Diana Baroni, Meredith McGinnis, Amanda O'Connor, Michael Nagin, Patricia Shaw, and Tammy Blake are the kind of people we writers cannot do without, and I fervently hope the book world realizes that for decades to come.

There are certain projects where the editor's contributions are especially crucial. This book was one of them, and my editor Gary Jansen altered tone, direction, and wording with astute judgment every step of the way—thank you. Our relationship has become one of trust, affection, and mutual respect.

My working existence is expertly guided by my staff Carolyn and Felicia Rangel, and Tori Bruce, who are as close as family. My thanks must also include Poonacha Machaiah, Sara Harvey, Kathy Bankerd,

Attila Ambrus, and the Chopra Center staff. You have all taught me what "the spirit in action" means.

My wife, Rita, is the light around which our extended family revolves. Now it embraces Mallika, Sumant, Tara, Leela, Gotham, Candice, and Krishu. They are the sweet joy of my life.